Biography — Truman

STEINBERG, Alfred

Harry S. Truman

DATE DUE

Biography — Truman

STEINBERG, Alfred
AUTHOR

Harry S. Truman
TITLE

DATE DUE	BORROWER'S NAME	ROOM NUMBER
FEB 6	Peter Stern	25
MAR 8	J. Ricciardi	22
DEC 6	L. D'Angelo	23

HARRY S. TRUMAN

Few Presidents have entered their tenure of office with graver crises in the United States and throughout the world than did Harry S. Truman. With the death of Franklin Delano Roosevelt, one of the most popular Presidents, people speculated about Harry Truman's ability to solve the problems facing the nation. In detail, Alfred Steinberg traces Harry Truman's life; the path which took him from a piano-playing boy in Independence, Missouri, to bank clerk, farmer, oil wildcatter, Captain Harry of Battery D, shopkeeper, savings and loan bank president, through the years as county judge, United States Senator, war program investigator, Vice-President and finally President.

HARRY S. TRUMAN

By

ALFRED STEINBERG

G. P. Putnam's Sons

New York

For Florence—for helping to interview Mr. Truman
and for other things too numerous to recount.

Library of Congress Catalog Card Number: 63-15554
Manufactured in the United States of America
Published simultaneously in the Dominion of Canada
by Longmans Canada Limited, Toronto
10216

CONTENTS

CONTENTS

HARRY S. TRUMAN

1

---•———◆———•---

BEGINNING OF THE ROAD

I̵t was early in May 1934 and Harry S. Truman had time to reflect on his life, as he briskly marched along the streets of Independence, Missouri, on his early-morning constitutional. In a few days he would be fifty years old and he had seemingly reached the end of the line of his minor political career. Twice he had won election as presiding county judge of Jackson County, on the western edge of Missouri. There was no chance to run again, for custom frowned on a third term. He had tried to win the backing of the local Democratic machine for a nomination to the U.S. House of Representatives. But this had quickly been denied him. The most he could hope for now, he concluded, was "retirement in some minor county office," as he sadly scrawled his prediction on a sheet of hotel stationery.

Yet in 1945, only eleven years later, this same man held the highest political office his nation could bestow upon any citizen—President of the United States. Since that day in

1934, he had traveled an amazing route, twice elected to the U.S. Senate and once to the Vice-Presidency. With the death of President Franklin D. Roosevelt in 1945, Truman spoke for the United States abroad, guided his nation's foreign relations, served as commander-in-chief of the armed forces, managed government agencies with more than two million employees, led a powerful political party, kept the public informed on a host of vital matters and promoted the national budget, tax program and hundreds of legislative measures through Congress each year.

Charlie Ross, the boyhood friend who later served as his White House press secretary, assessed his career in this fashion: "The rise of Harry Truman to the Presidency is one of the most amazing phenomena in American political history. Luck—or call it fate—time and time again intervened to send him down the right road when another road would have stopped him dead."

Only a few other successful political leaders in American history came face to face with political disaster as often as did Harry Truman. Yet against tremendous odds, he always managed to reach his goals. When he ran for his first office in 1922, he learned too late that the political bosses had agreed beforehand to support one of his opponents. Nevertheless, he did not drop out, but stepped up his campaign instead and emerged the victor.

When he ran for his last office in 1948, Democratic politicians told him to his face that he could not win the Presidential nomination from the Democratic National Convention. Later when he left the convention hall with the nomination, most delegates believed that he would be badly defeated by his Republican opponent in the general election that November. Even on election night when he enjoyed a wide lead, radio and television commentators assured the country that in the end he would be declared the loser.

Not long after Truman retired from politics in 1953, after almost eight years in the White House, admirers and even critics agreed that he had not only been badly underestimated as a politician but also as a statesman. In his terms as President, his decisions led to the development of the United Nations, the economic and military restoration of war-torn Western Europe through generous American aid, help to underdeveloped countries in Latin America, Africa and Asia, and to the start of the nuclear age.

Nevertheless, despite his achievements, no White House occupant in modern times underwent such continuous personal attacks as did Harry Truman. Some political opponents joked about his piano playing, even though he played the classics well. Others pointed out that he had begun his political career as a member of a local machine whose head eventually went to prison. Some mentioned at every opportunity that he could not possibly be a good President because he had failed in the haberdashery business as a young man. Others attacked him because of the loud sportshirts he wore on vacations, his frank speaking manner and his sharp letters to those who criticized his wife and daughter.

There were still others who tried to downgrade him because he did not stem from an elegant background of wealth. But Truman was proud of his ancestry of pioneers, soldiers and hard-working farmers. On his father's side, he could trace the family back to Joseph Truman, who migrated to the New World from Nottingham, England, in 1666. Joseph Truman was a carpenter, but he also found time to establish the family's great interest in politics by winning an election as constable in New London, Connecticut.

With the passage of years, the restless Truman clan spread southward into Virginia and then across the mountain gaps into the Kentucky wilderness. William Truman, Harry Truman's great-grandfather, served as a private in the Kentucky militia in the War of 1812. Afterward, he became a successful farmer and a popular citizen of Shelby County, where politics held second rank to religion as a topic of local interest.

It was his son, Anderson Shippe Truman, who extended the travels of the family when he moved westward to Missouri in 1846. Here on the western fringe, where the sandy Kaw met the chocolate Missouri River, he brought his bride, the former Mary Jane Holmes. Anderson Truman was a quiet and studious man whose profession was that of schoolmaster. However, to support his family of three daughters and two sons, he combined this activity with farming. The great stampede of covered wagons was already rolling westward into the vast Louisiana territory and the Southwest, recently acquired in the Mexican War. But Anderson Truman was too hard put eking out a bare livelihood to join the adventurous caravans. Moreover, Missouri was to his liking and here he chose to remain.

Of his five children, his favorite was his younger son, John Anderson Truman, born in 1851. As a youth, John revealed little of his father's studious nature. After only a few years at the local rural school, he quit to take on a man's work on the farm. He grew into a short, flat-skulled young man, noted in his neighborhood for his curious combination of good humor and fiery temper. He was also known as an outdoorsman and a lover of animals.

At the age of thirty, John Truman was still living with

his widower father on their poor 200-acre farm. But only three days before Christmas that year, John Truman took a bride, pretty Martha Ellen Young, the liveliest of neighbor Solomon Young's five daughters.

When Martha Young married John Truman in 1881, her father was considered a well-to-do man. He had spared no expense in providing her with an education, an unusual event for girls in those days, and she had attended a Baptist college for women, where she excelled in art and music. The bearded Solomon Young owned a fertile 600-acre farm at Grandview and a spacious house for his family of nine, plus servants, farmhands and visiting relatives. A handsome, muscular man, he had led an adventurous existence for twenty years as a wagon train master, running Conestoga trains westward across Indian prairies, the Rockies and the parched desert to the Pacific Ocean. Martha recalled her excitement as a child when he sat high over his lead 16-hitch ox team with his black snake whip poised for the start of another run over the magic West. Then came his shout of "Gee!" or "Haw!" and the wagon train rumbled out of civilization.

John Truman did not want anything from his father-in-law when he married Martha. With stubborn pride, the two climbed into a carriage following the wedding ceremony and headed south with little money. At Lamar, four counties below the Truman and Young farms and just north of the Ozarks, they decided to settle down. They found a small white house without a number on a street without a name. John Truman agreed to pay $685 for the property and the two moved in to begin married life. "Lamar was a pretty country village then," Martha later recalled. "It was built around a square with a courthouse in the center and elm and maple trees." Lamar was also the place where Wyatt Earp had begun his career as a constable only a few years earlier.

To support himself and Martha, John Truman went into business as a mule trader. The big barn behind the little house saw a steady trek of animals coming and going. Truman was an expert on animals and could tell a mule's age without examining its teeth. But he was up against shrewd, stubborn Missourians who considered bargaining half the fun of life.

By the spring of 1884, he was barely earning his daily bread but he had good reason for rejoicing. Martha was expecting a child.

On May 8, 1884, when she gave birth to a son, John Truman celebrated fatherhood by planting a pine tree near his wife's 6½-foot-wide bedroom. Afterward, he nailed a horseshoe over the front door to bring the infant good luck.

But all was not pure joy. The families back near Grandview argued as to the name to be given the child. John and Martha Truman had originally agreed to name a son Harrison Shippe Truman. The Harrison was to honor Martha's older brother, Harrison Young, while the Shippe was the middle name of John Truman's father, Anderson Shippe Truman. When the Youngs wanted the middle name changed to Solomon, after Solomon Young, Martha's father, the controversy was on.

Stubbornness on both sides prevented any settlement. Finally John Truman ended further debate by recording his son's name as Harry S. Truman. Thus did the infant who would one day become his nation's thirty-third President begin his existence.

2

---◆◆◆---

BOY OF INDEPENDENCE

By late 1885, when Harry Truman was a year old, his father's mule-trading business at Lamar became a losing proposition and the family moved to the village of Harrisonville, in the county directly below Kansas City. One of Harry's first memories was of relatives visiting at Harrisonville to see his new baby brother, Vivian, who was born in 1886. From the yard below came a loud greeting and, said Harry, "I remember when my mother dropped me from an upstairs window into the arms of my Uncle Harrison." There was another first memory of the elusive frog he chased around the yard. Whenever the frog leaped, the slender brown-haired boy with extremely white skin slapped his knees in sheer joy and laughed uproariously. He remembered that Grandmother Young, who was watching him, remarked afterward to his mother, "It's very strange that a two-year-old has such a sense of humor."

However, there was little cause for a display of humor at

that period. In 1887, his father's second attempt at animal swapping ended in failure and the family packed their few belongings and moved to the farm of his mother's parents at Grandview. To ease the situation somewhat, Grandfather Young declared himself too old to run the large farm and insisted that John Truman take over as manager. Then to add to John Truman's sense of failure, his father, who had moved with him onto the Young place, grew seriously ill. The seventy-one-year-old man did not last long and there came the night when he breathed his last while his three daughters stood about his bed. Little Harry, only three years old, so wanted to ease their suffering when he heard their sobbing that he rushed to his dead grandfather and pulled on his beard in a futile attempt to awaken him.

In 1889, when Harry's sister, Mary Jane, was born, the Young household was now a crowded establishment. Anderson Truman's will was probated and Harry's father decided to use his small inheritance to make a fresh start at independent family existence. His years of farming the 600 Young acres were not to his liking and he began a check of the surrounding area to find a likely place for resuming his animal-trading business.

By a process of elimination, John and Martha Truman decided on the town of Independence. Here was a thriving community of 6,000 persons, close to both the cattle center of Kansas City and the Young farm at Grandview. Moreover, Martha Truman concluded, her son Harry was so bright that he deserved the advantage of the excellent school system for which Independence was noted rather than the meager country schooling available at Grandview.

Harry was six when he moved to Chrysler Street in Independence across the way from the tracks of the Missouri-

Pacific Railroad. Even at that age he already possessed an insatiable interest in history, and he found that Independence was saturated in his country's history.

The town was part of Jackson County, established in 1827 by cheering supporters of "Old Hickory" Jackson, who believed he had been swindled out of the Presidency by John Quincy Adams three years earlier. Little Harry was swept along by the local pride in Andrew Jackson and began his lifelong interest in the seventh President and military hero.

There were other aspects of Independence's history that fascinated Harry. He learned, for instance, that Prophet Joseph Smith, the founder of the Mormon sect, had selected the town sixty years earlier as the New Zion of his church. But vicious mob violence broke out against the Mormons in the 1830's because of their peculiar religious practices, and in 1838 they were driven from the state. Harry's grandfather, Solomon Young, had once carried on business relations in the Utah Territory with the later Mormon leader, Brigham Young, and he told Harry that the Mormons had been badly treated in Missouri. "Don't think that only Baptists have free access to heaven," he warned his grandson.

Harry also discovered that Independence had served as the jumping-off spot for the Santa Fe and Oregon Trails. Grandpa Young described for him the scene of the 1840's when Smallwood Noland's Inn held 400 would-be pioneers and the tent camps held several hundred others waiting impatiently for the covered wagon treks to get under way. Independence was then acknowledged to be "the busiest town in America west of St. Louis." Later Harry thrilled to read the writings of historian Francis Parkman, who rode through Independence in 1846 and noted: "The town was crowded. The streets were thronged with men, horses and mules. A multitude of healthy children's faces were peeping out from under the cover of the wagons. The men, very sober-looking; among them some of the vilest outcasts in the country."

Still another feature of Independence's history, as Harry soon learned, was that the town had served as a center for the notorious Jesse James gang following the Civil War. Many of the local residents in town were personally acquainted with the outlaws, who began their wild careers with the first railroad robbery back in 1873. It was not until about the time of Harry's birth that the local county attorney successfully went after the gang as murderers and bandits. The Independence jailhouse even had a cell for Harry and his friends to stare into, one which once held Frank James prisoner.

Although the Civil War was now twenty-five years behind him, young Harry developed a strong sympathy for the Confederate cause from the stories his mother and Grandmother Young told him. One day in 1861, when Grandpa Young was on one of his Western journeys, they related to him, an unkempt man with wild hair came galloping into the Young acres, leading a hard-looking gang wearing red morocco leggings. This man was Jim Lane, then a United States Senator and boss of the Kansas Abolitionists, who were known as the "Red Legs" because of their attire.

All that morning, Lane had forced Grandma Young to bake biscuits and fry meat for his crew at gun point. Then Lane's gang shot 400 of Solomon Young's prize Hampshire hogs and chopped off solely the hams to carry away. "They shot our hens out of sheer cussedness, then they burned all our hay and set fire to our stock barns," Harry's mother described the pillage. "That wasn't all," Grandmother Young added to Harry. "They also stole the silverware and would have taken the big iron kettle and the rock crusher, but those were too blamed heavy."

Nor was this all. Two years later, Union General Thomas Ewing issued Order Number 11. This barred Confederate sympathizers from staying in many Missouri counties, including Jackson County where the Young homestead was. On a steaming afternoon, eleven-year-old Martha Young (Truman), her mother and five sisters and brothers filled an ox-cart and trudged behind it into an exile that lasted more than a year. It was natural that Martha Truman's bitterness should have impressed Harry.

Even though Martha Truman taught Harry to read at four, she did not send him to school until he was past eight. Just before the 1892 school term began, she made an appalling discovery. People had commented that his hazel eyes changed color according to his moods. But now she found him unable to recognize nearby objects, let alone small print. With great concern, she took him to a Kansas City oculist who noted that the boy suffered from flat eyeballs. (Normal eyeballs are convex, but Harry Truman's are flat as a table-top.) For the rest of his life he would have to wear extremely thick-lensed glasses and avoid the normal childhood games. "I was blind as a mole without them," Harry said.

His eye troubles were just one of a series of physical problems that befell him in his early years. Once, while combing his hair, he fell out of a chair and broke his collarbone. On another day he swallowed a peach stone and his breathing had almost stopped before his mother luckily pushed the pit down his throat with her fingers. Still another time he slammed the cellar door on his big toe and sliced off the end. A local doctor pressed the pieces together with crystalline iodoform and by some miracle, said Harry, "it stayed put and got well."

His most dangerous illness came when he was in the second grade. He and Vivian contracted diphtheria, and while Vivian recovered satisfactorily, Harry developed a paralysis of the legs and arms. For several months, the nine-year-old boy had to be wheeled outdoors in a baby carriage, until he suddenly regained the use of his limbs.

From the start, Harry's father did well in the animal-trading business. There were times, Harry recalled, when there were as many as 500 goats in the large fenced-in backyard on Chrysler Street. His father "never passed a cow," said Harry, "but what he stopped and tried to buy her." Business was so good that the family employed a housekeeper, "Auntie" Caroline Hunter. Harry was a boon companion of "Fat Sam" and little crippled Delsie, two of Auntie's five children, while Harry's father rented farmland south of town and worked it with Auntie's husband. John Truman also entered the real-estate business, drilled the first natural gas well in the area, and found time to invent an automatic railroad switch, though he failed to sell it to the Santa Fe Railroad.

Harry's bout with diphtheria had drawn him close to his mother, who felt the need to protect him. For the most part, she kept him indoors and taught him to cook and help out in the house. "Harry was 'old' even as a little boy," said a relative. He was especially attentive to his little sister, Mary Jane. Each night he sat her on his lap in the rocking chair and sang her to sleep. He also braided her hair and watched over her at play, with their pet dogs, cats, pigeons and pigs.

Although Vivian shared his father's interest in the outdoors and animals, nevertheless Harry had one chief interest in common with his father. This was in the field of politics. In 1892, John Truman was a loud supporter of the Democratic candidate for President, Grover Cleveland, when he ran against Benjamin Harrison. "I had a white cap with a visor on it saying 'Grover Cleveland and Adlai Stevenson' (grandfather of the contemporary Adlai Stevenson), the Democratic Presidential and Vice-Presidential candidates," Harry recalled. When the telegraphic report came declaring Cleveland the winner, he proudly watched his father ascend to the roof of the house and tie a large 44-star flag to the gilded rooster weather vane. In the victory torchlight parade, Harry thrilled at the sight of his father astride a tall gray horse.

John Truman took his politics seriously. In local election contests, he argued strenuously with Republicans at the courthouse square. Sometimes the arguments would turn into fist fights, and on occasion he would return home with his clothes torn and his body bruised. "If my father's honor was impugned," Harry observed, "he'd fight like a buzzsaw."

He remembered one time when his father was a witness in a case being tried in Judge James H. Slover's local courtroom. An unfriendly attorney, who weighed fifty pounds more than his father, was cross-examining him. John Truman had just finished answering a question when the lawyer leaned an elbow on the witness box, pointed a stiff finger in his face and bellowed, "Now, John, you know that's a lie!"

Harry's father leaped up and chased the lawyer from the court and down the street.

Five minutes later John Truman returned alone to the courtroom, Judge Slover leaned over the bench and inquired with a twinkle in his eyes, "Did you get him, John?"

"No, he got away," came the abject reply. "He ran inside a building across the street."

"Too bad," Judge Slover commiserated with him. "That fellow really had a good beating coming to him."

Harry was a secret admirer of his father's fighting prowess because he failed to have a single fist fight in all the years he was growing up. He was a bookish boy, made more so by his mother who bought books to occupy his time. When he was ten, she bought him four red volumes by Charles Francis Horne, titled *Great Men and Famous Women,* and these became his prize possession. In addition, he frequented the local public library, which contained about 5,000 volumes. "I read everything I could get my hands on—histories and encyclopedias and everything else," he said. There was hardly a book in the library that he did not read. By his twelfth birthday, he had finished his second careful reading of the Bible. "This was all to the good," said his mother, "for we all belonged to different churches in our family. There were Baptists, Presbyterians and Methodists. When anybody got into an argument, they always said Harry was best posted in the Bible, because he read all the history and the stories in it."

In 1896, John Truman concluded a profitable selling deal on his Chrysler Street property and the family moved to another house on Waldo Street, which at one time had been on the road leading to Independence's old river port. "We had a wonderful time in the neighborhood from 1896 to 1902," said Harry, referring to the "Waldo Street Gang." Nearby was a pond where the gang swam in the summer and skated in the winter. There was also a playing field for baseball and other games.

The Waldo Street Gang were fierce competitors, but Harry could not join in many of the games because of his glasses. His chief function was that of serving as umpire. There were the Allen brothers who later became nationally famous as basketball players and coaches. Besides Phog and Pete Allen, the gang included Elmer Twyman, later a physician; Charlie Ross, who became a top-rank newspaperman and Harry's White House press secretary; and three of the Wallace children—Frank, George and Bess.

Harry had met Bess, or Elizabeth Virginia Wallace, the first week he lived in Independence, when his mother sent him to Sunday school. From the start, he admired this small girl with blue eyes and golden curls, though, he recalled, "I didn't speak to her for five years." In the Waldo Street Gang, Bess was a tomboy excelling at all sports. Harry watched her skate on Bryant's pond, swat a baseball over the heads of fielders and whistle through her teeth. "From the fifth grade in school in her Aunt Nannie's class until my graduation from high school," Harry said, "we were in the same classes. If I succeeded in carrying her books to school or back home for her I had a big day."

There was more to his life at the time than serving as umpire to the Waldo Street Gang or gazing at Bess Wallace. When Harry was ten, his mother became his first piano teacher. When he showed first-class ability, she sent him for a while to a neighborhood teacher, then to Mrs. E. C. White, a Kansas City teacher who had studied under the renowned European master, Theodor Leschetizky, who had also instructed Jan Paderewski.

Twice a week Harry went to Mrs. White's rambling brick house for lessons, and he climbed out of bed each morning at five for two hours of practicing before going to school. Playing the piano was considered a sissy's activity by the boys in the neighborhood. "He didn't lack spunk," said Charlie Ross, "when he braved the jeers of the boys to go regularly to his music teacher, carrying his music roll."

He continued his lessons until he was fifteen. When he quit, both his mother and Mrs. White were dismayed because they believed he had real potential as a concert pianist. But, said Harry, "I missed being a musician, and the real and only reason I missed being one was because I wasn't good enough." However, his foundation was so excellent that he remained a rather good player of the classics in later life.

Besides playing the piano, when Harry reached his teens he and Vivian helped their father curry and water the horses, milk the cows and lead the goats to the public spring two blocks from the house. The boys were also responsible for weeding the vegetable patch and bringing in stove wood sawed by Old Rube, a crippled colored man. Through one entire night Harry rode horseback alongside his father while they herded cattle from Independence to the stockyard at Kansas City.

In the spring of 1898, when the United States declared war on Spain after the sinking of the battleship *Maine* in Cuba, Harry was determined to become a soldier. The Independence Junior Militia sprang into existence and he joined up. "There were a dozen or more of us, all in our early teens," he said, "and we liked to think we would join the armed forces in a unit if the Spanish-American War would only wait for us to get old enough."

The Junior Militia engaged in drilling exercises, camped out on the banks of the Little Blue River and practiced firing with their .22-caliber rifles. On the Fourth of July, the boys swaggered through town like veterans and listened to the Honorable Joe Upton of Bolivar as he delivered a patriotic oration. After the speech came the annual Fourth of July games. But the boys did not participate, said Harry, "because anything as undignified as chasing a greased pig was far beneath us."

When the Spaniards surrendered that summer, Harry returned to the less exciting life of a schoolboy in the fall. He now had his first paying job, earning three dollars a week at Jim Clinton's Drug Store on the town square. Here before school each morning, he swept the sidewalk, mopped the floor, washed the windows and dusted the counters, cases and drug bottles. "There must have been a thousand bottles to dust," he complained.

His next job came in 1900 when he worked as a page at the Democratic National Convention held in Kansas City. He delivered messages among the various delegations and listened to the speeches. The excitement of the Presidential nominating gathering thrilled him. "I remember that there were seventeen thousand people in the old convention hall when William Jennings Bryan spoke," he said. Bryan was then in the process of winning the second nomination of his three unsuccessful bids for the Presidency. "His appeal that day was like nothing I have ever heard. He had a bell-like voice that carried well and he knew how to use it."

Until the election contest ended that November, school did not seem so important to Harry. But when McKinley overwhelmed Bryan by an electoral count of 292 to 155, Harry's political excitement dimmed momentarily and he plunged back into his studies.

It was to be expected that a boy who was as voracious a reader as Harry would be a good student. From the time he read Appleton's *First Reader* in Miss Myra Ewing's first grade class at the South Side School until his graduation from high school in 1901, he took his schoolwork seriously. Yet from the beginning, his schoolmates found him an easy-going sort who smiled readily and engaged in occasional pranks. Mize Peters, who sat with him in a double seat, had an old Irish setter named Sam, who was the despair of the teachers because he sat outside the school all day long and barked. He stopped only during recesses when Harry and Mize entertained the other pupils by putting him through his tricks. Harry's best laugh-getter was to pretend that he had lost his balance. Old Sam, a sacrificing hound, would throw himself forward to break the fall with his own body.

On occasion, the boys skipped school, though Harry seldom engaged in this enterprise. Ringleader of the truants was Charlie Ross, son of the town jailer and later the high school valedictorian. One time the boys skipped school and were chased across the Missouri-Pacific tracks by the school janitor whose name was Speck. Speck failed to catch any of them, but in the chase Charlie fell on the cinders and suffered a deep nose cut. The boys were proud of him when he was called on to explain how he got his cut and he replied, "I leaned down to get a drink at the spring on Spring Street and a frog bit me in the nose."

Although Harry had started school two years behind his age group, nevertheless he was promoted rapidly and managed to finished high school at the age of seventeen. At that time few boys kept at their schooling until high school graduation. For instance, there were forty-one in Harry's graduation class, but only eleven were boys.

Harry's favorite subjects were history and Latin. During their spare time over a month, he, Charlie Ross and Elmer Twyman built a model bridge made precisely according to one of Caesar's bridges across the Rhine. "We found the description in the *Commentaries*," said Charlie. Harry was also active in the literary society and headed the debate team which took the positive position in the big debate on "Tariffs For Revenue Only." In class, whenever Harry rose to recite, he invariably squared his shoulders before speaking. When worried, he put his hand over his mouth. These were characteristics that were to remain with him. Charlie Ross, who was lanky and stoop-shouldered and whose expression was normally that of a sad hound dog despite his perennial good humor, always hung onto his desk and swayed as he spoke.

Latin also served to bring Harry into the company of Bess Wallace, his classmate. Twice each week he walked to the house on Delaware Street where his father's sister, Aunt Ella Noland, lived. Here he studied Latin with Bess and Cousins Ethel and Nellie. Aunt Ella soon noticed that he did little studying after Bess arrived. She said that she first became aware of Harry's silent attachment to Bess when he composed a piano piece. Bess was known for her special whistle for her closest friends and they, in turn, used another signal whistle in reply. The dominate theme of Harry's composition was the set of whistles arranged for the piano.

Miss Tillie Brown, who taught English, enjoyed relating stories about the Class of 1901. Her favorite pupil was Charlie Ross, with Harry a close second. Charlie was editor of the annual and Harry worked under him. At the graduation, Miss Tillie kissed only gangling Charlie. The other forty members of the class crowded around her and one boy asked, "Aren't you going to pass that around, Miss Tillie?" The frail teacher replied with the comment that she would kiss the others when they accomplished something worthwhile. "I hope yet to kiss a President of the United States," she said, certain that this was the most preposterous remark she could utter.

3

───◆◉◆───

BANK CLERK AND FARMER

MARTHA TRUMAN rewarded Harry for graduating high school by sending him on a trip that summer to visit relatives. He stayed for a short time with Grandma Young at Grandview and listened to the old lady's reminiscences. Grandpa Young had died in 1892 and the following year their large home had gone up in flames, due to the carelessness of a servant girl. The eighty-three-year-old woman was living in a small temporary residence on the property and she spoke eagerly to Harry about building another large house.

Next Harry journeyed away from home for the first time in his life to spend some time with Aunt Ada, the youngest of his grandmother's five daughters, who lived at Murphysboro, Illinois, and loved to play euchre. After endless sessions of these card games with Aunt Ada, he went on to stay with his mother's Aunt Hettie in St. Louis. As a boy, Harry had traveled in a cart with two high wheels to the Belton

Fair with Grandpa Young, who served as a judge of the horse races. Now in St. Louis, he went to the race track with Great Aunt Hettie's son. Here, to show he was a man, yet with great reluctance, he bet five dollars on a horse. His inner voice was filled with confusion about the evils of gambling when his horse won and he collected $125. But despite the joy at his gain, he never bet on a horse race again throughout his life.

His mother's lighthearted mood had disappeared by the time he returned home. Martha Truman had looked forward to sending Harry to college that fall. Down the street Charlie Ross already had his suitcase to carry his clothes to Columbia, where he planned to enter the University of Missouri to study journalism; and Elmer Twyman would soon be off to college to follow in his father's footsteps at medical school. But Mrs. Truman's dream of a college education for her son was now shattered.

The trouble lay in her husband's business reverses. Not content with his various enterprises, John Truman had speculated heavily in the Kansas City grain market future. By early 1901, he had been worth about $30,000. But suddenly the market collapsed, and, said Harry, "He lost everything at one fell swoop and went completely broke."

Despite his father's situation, Harry made his own effort to gain a free college education. Miss Maggie Phelps, his high school history teacher, agreed to tutor him and Fielding Houchens, son of a local preacher, for the coming exams for West Point and Annapolis. Harry studied eagerly with Miss Maggie until one day when he stopped in at an Army recruiting station in Kansas City. He was told bluntly that he could not qualify for West Point because of his eyes.

By the fall of 1901, Harry's help was needed to keep the

family going. After a search for available jobs, he found employment with a contractor named L. J. Smith, who was building local trackage for the Santa Fe Railroad. Six days a week and at a salary of $35 a month, Harry's job was to maintain time records for 400 gandy dancers, or railroad hoboes, whom Smith hired for track work. Twice daily, Harry had to pump a handcar to each of Smith's three camps to fill out time tickets for the grading laborers. At night he had to sleep with the gandy dancers in their foul tents and eat their grubby food. Their language was unprintable, but Harry tried to reassure himself that he was seeing a section of life that was educational for a boy with high ideals. Every other Saturday evening he had to go to the saloons in Independence and Sheffield to pay the men, who drew about eleven dollars for two weeks' work. He knew that as soon as they had their wages, the gandy dancers would drink away their earnings and report back to work penniless on Monday. Despite the degrading association, by the time Smith's contract ended in June 1902, Harry believed he had "received a very down-to-earth education in the handling of men."

At this point, his father desperately needed cash to stave off complete ruin. He had sold the 160-acre farm Solomon Young had bequeathed to Martha Truman, a farm that had been in the family for a half century. His only remaining possibility for cash was a 40-acre farm he had bought sight unseen in Oregon County in southern Missouri. "We crossed a little river by fords, thirteen times in eight miles," Harry reported on their ride to the farm. "We found the forty acres running up the side of an Ozark mountain. It wasn't worth a nickel."

Once they returned home, Harry took a job for a short

time as a $7-a-week wrapper in the mailing room of the Kansas City *Star*. Meanwhile, his father sold the Waldo Street house and retained only enough money to make a small down payment on a cheap, little house at 2108 Park Avenue in Kansas City. Then to eat, he took a dismal job as nightwatchman with the Missouri Elevator Company in Kansas City. He was fifty-one now, and his dream of becoming a wealthy man was gone forever.

Not long afterward, Harry and Vivian became bank clerks with the Kansas City National Bank of Commerce. Harry's starting salary was $35 a month, and he worked in what was known as the "zoo," or the caged section in the bank's damp basement which served as the clearinghouse for checks drawn on banks in rural areas. All day long he sat on a stool and made notations in longhand. The job was unbearably dull and he complained to a fellow employee, "I don't have enough responsibility. I don't have anything to decide." Nor were there adequate opportunities for advancement. "The bank's vice-president would always remember a trivial mistake when a clerk asked for a raise," said Harry.

In 1904, he celebrated his twentieth birthday by moving to the Union National Bank as a $60 a month bookkeeper. At this time also his mother insisted that it was time he was baptized and he became a member of the Baptist Church, even though he frankly told her, "All the religion I have is found in the Ten Commandments and the Sermon on the Mount."

Harry was also on his own for the first time when his father sold the Kansas City house and bought an 80-acre farm near the town of Clinton. At first, Harry lived with Aunt Emma Colgan, one of his father's sisters. Then in 1905 he moved to Mrs. Trow's boardinghouse on Troost Avenue.

One of his fellow boarders was another bank clerk named Arthur Eisenhower who came from Abilene, Kansas. Arthur's younger brother was a fifteen-year-old boy named Dwight D. Eisenhower.

"Harry and I only had a dollar a week left over for riotous living," Arthur Eisenhower later said, recalling life at Mrs. Trow's place. But Harry knew how to stretch his pennies. He was the piano accompanist for the frequent evening songfests in the house and he and Arthur went on picnics with Mrs. Trow's daughter, Ida, and her pretty friend, Casby Bailey.

Harry managed not only to get by on his salary but also to send money to his parents. Mrs. Trow provided him with a room and two meals a day for $5 a week. He spent only ten cents for lunch and ate it at a nickel movie. On Saturdays he worked as an usher at the Grand Theater and enjoyed a free showing of such well-known vaudeville acts as George M. Cohan, Lillian Russell and the Floradora Girls. During the classical concert series at the old convention hall, he bought the cheapest top gallery seat.

There was also a necessary twenty-five-cent expenditure each week. On Flag Day in 1905, Battery B of the Missouri National Guard was organized and he became a charter member. Battery B met once a week at the local armory where each man paid a quarter for the privilege of drilling. Harry started as a private and No. 2 man on the 3-inch light gun, learned jujitsu, fencing and the art of handling Army horses before he left the Guard after two three-year hitches.

He was especially proud of his blue dress uniform, and one time he wore it on a visit to Grandma Young. "This is the first blue uniform to enter this house since the War

Between the States!" she scolded him. "Don't you ever come here wearing it again, Harry."

While Harry was making his way as a bank clerk, John Truman failed again. He had hoped to begin anew at the Clinton farm, but unfortunately a flood washed away his entire corn crop. There was little else for him and his wife to do except to move back to the Young farm. Not long afterward he requested Harry to quit his bank job to manage the Young farm, and in the summer of 1906 Harry returned to Grandview.

This abrupt change in Harry's life was to his liking. During the next ten years he rose each morning at 4:30 A.M. in the summer and at 6:30 in the winter. Almost without end, it seemed to him, he "plowed, sowed, reaped, milked cows, fed hogs, doctored horses, baled hay and did everything there was to do on a 600-acre farm." His mother claimed that he planted the straightest row of corn in the entire county. "I had to," Harry admitted, "for if I didn't my father would force me to hear about it for a whole year afterward."

The Young farm was especially fertile. It held broad wheat and corn fields, pasture land, vegetable gardens, orchards and watermelon patches, besides the plentiful animals. Nevertheless, Harry added to production by crop rotation, soil conservation practices and continual weed fighting. He was the first farmer in that area to stack hay with a derrick and swing, as well as being the local innovator of the practice of vaccinating hogs against cholera. Many of his neighbors scoffed at his attempt to maintain records of actual cost per acre for his various crops. Others derided his use of labor-saving implements instead of hiring more farmhands. Still others questioned his feeding methods for hogs until he told them, "Go ahead and continue to raise the lard, and I'll raise the meat."

Others insisted nothing would come of his efforts because the Young farm was jinxed. This began when a woman visitor broke her leg when her carriage overturned on the farm. Then one day when John Truman was putting head-gear on a mule, the animal yanked a piece of timber free and broke his leg. Harry was next when a calf ran into him in the spring of 1913 and broke his leg. Brownie Huber, one of his farmhands, said, "Harry just took it kind of easy and grinned, and kidded the neighbors who came to see him."

With Harry running the farm, John Truman felt free to spend his time at his chief interest and was soon busily involved in local politics. When he won appointment as elec-tions judge in the Grandview precinct in 1906, Harry took on his first political job by serving as his clerk. Two years later John Truman served as a county delegate to the Mis-souri State Democratic Convention at Joplin. Afterward came an appointment as a road overseer in the Eastern Dis-trict of Jackson County. This meant that he would keep watch on the local Democrats, as well as collect taxes and boss a crew repairing bridges and culverts and leveling the dirt roads.

So life proceeded until 1909 when Grandma Young, who was born in 1818, celebrated her ninety-first birthday. But hardly a month passed before she took ill and died. Her will cut off five of her children with only five dollars apiece and gave her farm, estimated to be worth $150,000, to her daugh-ter Martha and her son Harrison. The four daughters and the son who were cut off immediately began legal action that lasted a decade. Harry's mother agreed to pay them a great deal of money in exchange for their quitclaims. But in doing so she had to borrow money from the bank and ended up saddled with large mortgages.

There was more personal misfortune during this period. Although the average road overseer did no physical work for his salary, John Truman was different. In the summer of 1914 he was inspecting a road and found a boulder barring traffic. Instead of asking one of the young road workers to push the boulder off the road, he foolishly did it himself. That night he suffered from severe stomach pains and by morning he had difficulty breathing. Finally Harry hitched up the buggy and took him to a Kansas City hospital where he was operated on for an intestinal block.

He seemed well on the mend when he returned home that fall. Harry spent a great deal of time at his bedside talking to him. One evening in November, Harry came in from his farm chores and took the chair next to his father's bed. "I had been sitting with him and watching a long time," he said. "Then I fell asleep for a short time and when I woke up he was dead."

4

OIL OPERATOR

His father's death made Harry Truman the head of the household. He was thirty now and ran not only the 600-acre farm but also another 300-acre farm owned by his Uncle Harrison.

However, he possessed too much energy to restrict himself even to the onerous farm duties. He found time to organize the Jackson County Farm Bureau and the first boys and girls farm club in western Missouri. In addition, he became interested in the Masonic order and formed Grandview Lodge No. 618. He also took over his father's old post as road overseer of Washington Township. This did not last long, however, because he proposed a major road overhaul and his political superiors refused permission. In 1915, he also became postmaster of Grandview. The job paid $50 a month, which he turned over in its entirety to his assistant, Ella Hall.

There was still another major developing interest. One evening he rode horseback into Independence and paid a call on Aunt Ella, Cousin Nellie and Cousin Ethel. That morning a neighbor had sent a cake to the Nolands. After Harry took the last piece, Aunt Ella washed the cake plate and asked Nellie to return it to Mrs. Wallace across the street. When Harry heard the Wallace name mentioned, he insisted on returning the cake plate and said he would be right back.

It was not until two hours later that he returned. "Thanks for returning the cake plate," Aunt Ella said with dry amusement.

"Well, I saw Bess," Harry announced with a broad grin. Thus began his courtship of Bess Wallace.

Much had happened to Bess since Harry had seen her last at the 1901 high school graduation. Bess had lived at 610 Delaware at that time but now she lived with her widowed mother and three brothers at her grandparents' home at 219 Delaware Street, across the narrow street from Aunt Ella.

Harry remembered her father, David W. Wallace, as a tall handsome man with long sideburns and a heavy mustache. He had such a pleasing personality that at the young age of thirty-one he became the Eminent Commander of the Knights Templar of Missouri. But outside of his Masonic leadership, he never seemed to be able to advance himself in the business world. For a time he had been the deputy county recorder in charge of issuing marriage licenses at the creaking Independence courthouse. Later he worked for the U.S. Customs Office in Kansas City. Then at the age of forty-three, in 1903, he died.

Bess's mother, Madge Gates Wallace, held the reputation as the "queenliest woman Independence ever produced." Harry knew of the local gossip which reported that she never wore a housedress and that few in town did not shrink from her withering glance. Mrs. Wallace's father, George Gates, who had come to Independence by way of Vermont, was

considered the leader of local society as well as the richest
man in town. Mr. Gates was the manufacturer of Queen of
the Pantry Flour, a well-known Midwest product which he
advertised as the source of "The Best Biscuits In The
World." In the same year that Lincoln was assassinated,
George Gates built his large woodframe house on Delaware
Street and here his widowed daughter had brought her
family.

Mr. Gates wanted only the best for his granddaughter.
The year after Bess moved in with him and his wife, he
sent her to the Barstow School for Girls in Kansas City. Although this was a finishing school to turn out socially adept
young women, Bess excelled in sports during her years there.
In voluminous blue-serge bloomers and white middy blouse,
the customary attire of girl athletes in those days, she won
the shot-put contest in the school's annual field day. She
was also the star forward who led the Barstow basketball
team to a 22–10 victory over the Independence girls' team.
When her grandfather bought the first Studebaker in Independence, he taught her how to drive. She also owned a handsome black horse and walked two sleek greyhounds through
the town's streets.

When Harry began courting Bess, he found that his friends
did not take him seriously. One pointed out that only a male
athlete would interest her. Indeed a recent beau had been
dropped because of his poor ability on the tennis court.
Harry was also aware that her grandfather and her mother
did not approve of him. As one of his friends put it, "Harry
was about the most unpromising prospect for a husband we
had around here then." He had no money in the bank, no
college education and no future. No one believed Mrs. Wallace would consent to her daughter marrying a dirt farmer,
one who did not even own the farm he toiled upon.

Despite these drawbacks, Harry was intent on making her his bride. The trip from Grandview to Independence was a long one, yet Harry found every excuse to come the twenty miles into town to see her. Sometimes he came on horseback. Other times he drove a horse and buggy to Dodson and then rode the trolley an hour and a half into Independence. His friend, Mize Peters, recalled that one Sunday Harry's horse reared up en route and overturned the buggy into a ditch. "Harry wasn't hurt, but he was furious because his clothes were ruined," said Peters.

During the week he wrote Bess frequently. Years later he found Bess burning papers on the hearth. When he inquired as to the nature of the papers, she told him, "I'm burning your letters to me."

"Bess!" he told her, "you oughtn't to do that."

"Why not?" she replied. "I've read them several times."

"But think of history!" he protested.

"I *have*," said Bess wryly.

Despite the opposition of her family, Bess found Harry's company enjoyable, even though they were opposites in many respects. She liked to fish, dance, play High Fives, the current card game, and go to baseball games. He found all these activities boring. Not only was he unable to dance but he was unwilling to learn. He enjoyed talking about history and battles and could go on for hours detailing the virtues and faults of the likes of Genghis Khan, Frederick the Great, Caesar, Gustavus Adolphus, George Washington, Napoleon, Robert E. Lee and Stonewall Jackson. He also enjoyed talking about serious music and playing the piano for hours at a time. But they both liked picnics, vaudeville shows and concerts. One thing they had in common was that they both loved to tease and rib each other constantly.

The time came when he had the opportunity to simplify his travel problem and impress Mr. and Mrs. George Gates and Mrs. Wallace. He was able to do this by purchasing a shiny four-door touring car for $600. A new Stafford sold for $2,350 and though Harry's car was secondhand it was in excellent condition. Before long, he was pulling up at 219 North Delaware to pick up Bess, her brothers George and Frank and their girl friends, and shoot into the countryside at sixty miles an hour to a choice picnic site. Several of Harry's friends agreed that the frosty attitude of the older generations in Bess's family melted to some extent because of his Stafford.

After his father died in 1914, Harry was anxious to make himself financially independent so that Bess's family would take him seriously. If he were to build up a bank account it would have to come through some enterprise other than farming his mother's and uncle's farms, even though he loved farming. "Riding one of those plows all day, day after day," he said, "gives one time to think. I settled all the ills of mankind in one way or another riding along."

But riding a plow year in and year out did not settle his own personal problem. A gauge of his own lack of progress was that Charlie Ross was now a professor of journalism at the University of Missouri and Elmer Twyman was well established as a physician.

Early in 1915, he ran across Jerry Culbertson, who had served as prosecuting attorney in nearby Cass County. Culbertson was now a glib-talking mining promoter and had so far promoted several gold mines, none of which had ever paid off. In a loud, enthusiastic manner, Culbertson proceeded to tell Harry about one of his current propositions, a lead and zinc mine situated at Commerce, Oklahoma, just south of the Missouri border. The mine was supposed to be played out, Culbertson said with a wink, adding confidentially that it actually contained rich veins of ore that the previous owners had overlooked.

Harry scraped together $2,000, as did Tom Hughes, his neighbor, and together the two took possession of this seemingly profitable mine. A quick trip to Commerce revealed enormous excitement among the mining interests there because the outbreak of the European War in 1914 had brought a steep, rising demand for lead and zinc. The two partners soon had their mine in operation, hopeful that they might make the millions that came from the nearby famous Turkey Fat Mine at an earlier era.

Each week Harry commuted between the farm and the mine. Later he said, "I undertook to run it along with a red-haired hoisting engineer by the name of Bill Throop, but we couldn't make our mine pay." Months of effort produced only enormous piles of slag and chat (waste rock). Throop admired Harry's industry and he asked him to raise another $2,500 to buy a drilling machine "and go up north of Picher, Oklahoma, and prospect the land up there for lead and zinc." But Harry had already lost his $2,000 at Commerce and could not raise the additional $2,500. Not long afterward he heard that other prospectors discovered enormous amounts of lead and zinc at Picher. "If I had done it we'd be rolling in wealth," he said ruefully.

In 1916, Uncle Harrison died and his will bequeathed his half-interest in the Grandview farm to Martha Truman, Harry, Vivian and Mary Jane. Harry was now a fairly prosperous property owner in his own right, but he still had no cash.

Shortly after Uncle Harrison's death, Jerry Culbertson visited the farm and expressed his sadness to Harry because the Commerce mine hadn't panned out. But he had a new sure-fire proposition, he insisted, that would make Harry wealthy. This time he proposed that Harry enter the oil-drilling business with him and an experienced oilman named David Morgan. Culbertson said that if Harry came into the deal Culbertson would be willing to contribute his promotional skills in exchange for a third of the profits. Morgan had agreed to put 1,500 acres of land he owned in eastern Oklahoma into the business, and Harry could become a partner by contributing $5,000 for working capital.

Harry threw caution to the wind and agreed to help form this new firm of Morgan & Company. "I was sucker enough to get into it," he said. Since he lacked the cash, he took out a $5,000 loan, agreeing to repay this amount in ten months. An embarrassing moment came when the lender refused to give him the money in his own signature, but insisted that the "notes shall also be signed by Martha E. Truman, the mother of said Harry S. Truman."

Under the business contract he became treasurer of the company, Morgan, the president, and Culbertson, secretary. Morgan was soon traveling about the country, checking and leasing oil properties and bossing the drilling of test oil wells. Besides keeping the money records, Harry assisted Morgan at their numerous meetings with lease owners, salesmen, drillers and other oil scouts. A flurry of business developed because hundreds of other wildcatters had suddenly grown aware of the vast oil market for the booming, new automobile business.

The company began earning a small profit and Harry had no trouble meeting payment on his notes. However, the business was so risky that at any time the partners might be wiped out. Morgan once described Harry's energetic efforts and enthusiasm to keep the business going in this fashion, "Harry was greatly interested in the oil development business. He liked the element of chance (he called it hazard)."

Harry soon found out how much hazard and chance were involved. Morgan & Company leased land in Louisiana, for instance. On the adjoining lot, the Standard Oil Company produced a thousand barrels of oil a day. But the Morgan lot, said Harry, "drew some of the finest salt water in the entire area." Company profits came from the manipulation of leases, buying them at low prices and selling them at higher prices. The test wells they sank, Harry recalled, "unfortunately proved to be dry holes."

Nevertheless, the company progressed and at the beginning of April, 1917, a large ad in the Kansas City *Star* notified readers that the company would sell to the public 10,000 shares of common stock at $25 a share. The ad referred to Harry Truman as a "native of Jackson County, Missouri; widely known in Kansas City."

But time was rapidly running out for Truman. On April sixth Congress declared war on Germany and World War I was on, so far as the United States was concerned. Truman realized that his first duty was to his country.

"At the time the war came," he said, "we had a well down nine hundred feet on a 320-acre lease at Eureka, Kansas." Truman was no longer on the scene when Morgan stopped drilling and sold the lease to another company. "They drilled a well down deeper," Truman said, "and there was never a dry hole found on those 320 acres. It was the famous Teeter Pool." Morgan estimated that if he had only continued drilling another nine hundred feet, he and Harry would have been millionaires. Instead this fortune went to the succeeding firm, the Empire Company, which later became known as the Cities Service Oil Company.

After Truman became President, he wrote to Morgan, "Maybe I wouldn't be Pres if we'd hit."

5

CAPTAIN HARRY
OF BATTERY D

Since the beginning of 1917, argument had raged in Washington whether to expand the National Guard units in the various states into combat divisions or to put all effort into building up the regular Army. Persuasive talk by Major Douglas MacArthur, who, as assistant to Secretary of War Newton D. Baker, championed the National Guard, evoked a favorable decision from President Wilson.

Shortly after the United States declared war on Germany on April 6, 1917, Truman ran into Major John L. Miles in Kansas City. Miles had commanded Independence's Battery C of the Missouri National Guard at the Mexican border in 1916 under General John J. "Black Jack" Pershing during the border troubles with Mexico's Pancho Villa. Miles told Truman that the Missouri National Guard planned to expand into two regiments, one for each end of the state.

Battery B of Kansas City and Battery C of Independence were to be expanded into a six-battery outfit called the 2nd Missouri Field Artillery.

When Miles asked Truman to join up and help him recruit others to activate the 2nd, Truman hesitated only momentarily. His mother's mortgages on the Grandview farm totaled $25,000. Moreover, he was still managing the farm, combining that labor with his duties in the oil business. But patriotism won out and he agreed to join up. His eyes were too poor to meet minimum Army requirements, but a helpful recruiting sergeant winked away his shortcoming and he was quickly sworn into service.

When he went home and broke the news, he said, "It was quite a blow to my mother and sister." His brother Vivian, who was the father of twins, lived on a nearby farm and lacked time to manage his mother's place. However, Mary Jane was now twenty-eight and Harry arranged for his sister to run the farm with the help of farmhands.

When he told Bess Wallace what he had done, she wanted to get married without delay. But he insisted that it was wiser to wait until after the war. For if he came home a cripple, he said, he did not want to tie her down. Instead, they immediately announced their engagement.

Recruiting went on at a busy pace at the old convention hall in Kansas City. Truman not only helped raise a supply and headquarters company for the 2nd Missouri Field Artillery but he also worked hard to raise a battery for the St. Louis National Guard regiment. Enthusiasm and patriotism engulfed the city and Truman felt he belonged—as he had never belonged before.

In those days enlisted men elected their officers when new military units were formed. Truman and his boyhood friend,

Harry "Pistol Pete" Allen, were in Battery F, and the battery elected Allen its captain. Truman hoped that Allen would name him a sergeant, but the battery did more than this for him. When the votes for lesser officers were counted, he found himself a first lieutenant.

On August 5, 1917, the 2nd Field Artillery was sworn into the regular Army and became the 129th Field Artillery of the 35th Division. Then on September 26, Truman and his buddies in the 129th marched through Kansas City in a heavy rain and boarded trains for Camp Doniphan located at Fort Sill, Oklahoma.

Here at the edge of the Witchita Mountains began the slow process of developing a battle-readiness division. Not only did Truman attend military instruction classes but he also took his regular turn as officer of the day, horsemanship officer and firing-instruction officer of Battery F.

He had still another duty on top of these. Colonel Karl D. Klemm, who was in charge of the 129th, ordered him to serve as regimental canteen officer. Truman knew nothing about running a store, so he chose Edward Jacobson, an enlisted man with previous merchandising experience, to assist him. They began operations by collecting two dollars from each of the 1,100 men of the 129th. Then they spent most of the $2,200 buying supplies at Oklahoma City. Next they started a barber and tailor shop and stocked their post exchange with items such as cigarettes, clocks and pens, which were not government issue. For clerks, they requisitioned a man from each battery and company, and to make certain there would be no stealing, Truman and Eddie Jacobson sewed up the pockets of their clerks and deposited their sales intake daily.

Business was brisk for most items, but where goods moved

slowly Truman and Jacobson devised special selling techniques. "Lieutenant Truman had some sweaters that weren't moving," said Captain Harry Jobes of the 129th. "One day he passed word around that he was doing us all a special favor with an unusual bargain in sweaters at six dollars each. We mobbed the canteen like women at a piece-goods sale. Later when I audited the books, I found those sweaters had cost him only three dollars each."

All other canteens at Fort Sill showed heavy losses, but Truman's did so well that after only six months he paid back the $2,200 investment and posted a profit of $15,000, or a dividend of 666 percent.

Brigadier General Lucien G. Berry, a martinet of the old Army school who ran Camp Doniphan, believed that the proper approach in directing his men was to find fault with whatever they did. He would order a three o'clock officers' call, arrive at 2:30 and scold everyone who appeared after he came for tardiness. When Captain Allen sent Berry a glowing report recommending Truman's promotion to captain, Berry scrawled out a rejecting reply, "There isn't anybody that good." Berry finally agreed to examine Truman for promotion in February 1918. On the appointed day he kept Truman waiting an hour outdoors with the temperature at −10 degrees, and after he cross-examined the candidate he scratched his handlebar mustache and bellowed, "I thought you were an ignorant rookie! It will be a disaster to the country to let you command men!" Nevertheless, in April he approved Truman's captaincy.

At one officers' call, Berry expressed great shock that he had found some waste paper on the floor in Truman's canteen. He was in the midst of a scolding torrent when loud, laughing voices from outdoors interrupted him. Then through the doorway sauntered four officers who froze at the sight of the general. "What is your name, mister?" Berry screamed at the largest officer.

"Lieutenant Vaughan, sir. Harry Vaughan." Berry wanted to know how long he had been an officer and he replied quivering, "Three days, sir."

Berry proceeded to give Vaughan a dressing-down that lasted several minutes. "Meanwhile," said Vaughan, "Truman stepped back into the ranks and made himself thin. And when the meeting was over, he joined me as we were leaving. 'Thanks a lot, mister,' he told me. 'You got me off the hook.'" This began an important relationship between both men.

While Truman was at Camp Doniphan, he wrote each day to Bess Wallace. On occasion his mother and sister came to visit him. He learned afterward that while his mother smiled in his presence and told him of her pride in him, "she cried all the way home."

In early March, Truman got his orders to leave Camp Doniphan in a group of ten officers and a hundred men for special artillery instruction in France. He was on his way east on March 20 when he persuaded a railroad employee at Rosedale, Kansas, to let him use the company phone to call Bess. "If she doesn't break the engagement at four o'clock in the morning, she really loves you," the switchman told him.

Once on the East Coast, he spent most of a 24-hour leave in New York buying three extra pairs of glasses. Then on March 30, he walked up the gangway of the *George Washington* with 7,000 others heading for the battle fronts in Europe. He debarked at Brest, France, and caught the train for Montigny-sur-Aube, where he was put through quick but rigid training for five weeks on French .75-mms. guns mounted on high wheels. He read in *The New York Times* that his promotion to captain came through on April 23 and he added another bar on his shoulder insignia. However, official word of the promotion did not reach him until October and when he asked for retroactive pay, his claim was not allowed on the ground that he had not "accepted" his commission earlier!

While he underwent special training on French guns, the 129th arrived in France. Now as captain and adjutant of the 129th's Second Batallion, he accompanied the outfit to Angers in Brittany for extra training at Camp Coetquidan, which he fondly recalled from his boyhood reading as an old Napoleonic artillery camp.

Two special events occurred at Camp Coetquidan. First he met Captain John W. Snyder of the 57th Field Artillery of the 32nd "Red Arrow" Division. Their acquaintance was to develop into a close personal association in the years to come.

The second important event took place on July 11. Battery D of the Second Battalion was known as an untamed, unmanageable outfit that had already run through three commanding officers. "Dizzy D," as it was called, consisted of 188 men, most of whom hailed from the rough neighborhood around Rockhurst College, a Jesuit school in Kansas City. At Camp Doniphan and all the way to France, the men fought and played infantile tricks on other batteries. At Camp Doniphan, the rule was to avoid the men with the bay-colored horses. The batteries there were distinguishable by the color of their horses: Battery A had only black horses; B, dark brown; C, light brown; D, bay (dull brown, red-yellow); E, sorrel; and F, black-white-gray horses.

Colonel Klemm called Truman in and told him to take

over Battery D on July 11. That first day the men faked a stampede of their 167 horses; and in the evening they staged a barroom brawl in their bunkhouse, breaking chairs and cots and necessitating the hospitalization of four men.

In the morning Truman called in his noncommissioned officers. "Men," he told the corporals and sergeants, "I know you've been making trouble for your previous commanders. From now on you're going to be responsible for maintaining discipline in your squads and sections. And if there are any of you who can't, speak up now and I'll bust you back right now."

In the weeks that followed, Truman tried to show Dizzy D that he meant to be boss, though he admitted he feared they would see through his falsely harsh expression. "I'd get myself back of a table and look as mean as I could," he said. Once when one of the men complained endlessly about the cooking, Truman ended the talk by ordering the man to take charge of the mess duty.

There was, of course, a bitter war raging on the battlefields while all this was going on. The objective of the German High Command that spring and early summer was to end the war before General Pershing could add his 2,000,000 American doughboys to the British and French troops barring the road to Paris. While Truman was still trying to browbeat his way to control of Dizzy D, the Germans inaugurated a massive attack in the Champagne-Marne area, a short distance from the French capital, on July 14, 1918. This drive was halted by French General Henri Gouraud, with the aid of the American Rainbow Division.

Afterward, more divisions of the American Expeditionary Force (A.E.F.) were dispatched to the fronts and in mid-

August the 129th Field Artillery got its marching orders, to proceed to France's northeast.

Captain Truman had his men high in the Vosges Mountains on Mount Herrenberg in Alsace, by reputation a quiet sector. On the night of September 6, he received orders to fire a barrage at the enemy. What resulted became known as "The Battle of Who Run."

First, Truman's four guns poured 500 rounds into the German lines. But now the enemy's bombs began exploding close to Dizzy D and a sergeant screamed, "Run, boys, they got a bracket on us!"

The men panicked and all but a few fled into the forest. Truman was so enraged by their flight that he "called them everything I knew." Father Curtis Tiernan, the regiment's Catholic chaplain, described what followed: "Captain Truman's words took the skin off the ears of those boys. It turned those boys right around." They crept back, crestfallen, to take their positions on the line.

There was no question after the Battle of Who Run that Truman was the boss of Battery D. Colonel Klemm insisted that he court-martial the sergeant who had brought about the stampede to the rear. But Truman refused to do this on the ground that it resulted from his first experience under fire. Instead, he "busted" him back to private and shipped him off to another battery.

Shortly afterward, General Pershing ordered the 35th Division to quit the Vosges sector and march to the Saint-Mihiel front. For the first time an army composed only of American divisions was to face the enemy. Since 1914, the Germans had held a triangular spearhead twenty-five miles long and about fifteen miles wide deep inside the French lines defending Paris. This spearhead was of great importance to the Germans, for if they lost this land peninsula they would no longer be able to protect Metz, their key road, rail and communications center. Marshal Ferdinand Foch, the Allied Commander, hoped that the A.E.F., inexperienced as it was, would liberate this area in northeastern France and push the Germans back to the so-called Hindenburg Line at the base of the triangle.

Pershing planned to surprise the Germans in the Saint-Mihiel triangle. Orders went out to the 35th Division to travel only by night and hide in the woods during the day to avoid German air observation. This was a difficult march because of the deep mud all along the route. One night a regimental commander didn't like the looks of Truman's tired men straggling over a hill. "Order those men to close ranks and march on the double," he bellowed. Instead, Truman lead his men off the road and told them to bivouac to regain strength. This action did much to win him complete loyalty from his men.

Fierce fighting broke out against the head of the triangle on September 12 and continued for eight days. Acknowledged hero of the battle was Brigadier General Douglas MacArthur of the 42nd Rainbow Division.

Afterward, Truman's battery and the rest of the 35th Division moved to the wooded plateau Meuse-Argonne sector, where a million American doughboys from 27 divisions attempted to smash the enemy's last stronghold along the Hindenburg Line.

When the military train pulled into a siding, Truman jumped off and was met by a tall, beefy lieutenant colonel, who introduced himself as Bennett Clark of Missouri, the son of the Speaker of the House of Representatives. Clark pointed at two dead horses lying close by and warned Truman to unload and get his men under cover quickly. "The Huns are putting down a prohibitive shelling here every hour on the hour," he said.

Truman worked his men frantically unhitching their horses, guns and ammunition. When more than an hour passed, he walked back to the station and confronted Clark, who was grinning broadly. "The joke's on you," Clark haw-hawed. "The Germans haven't fired here at all." To Truman's angry inquiry about the dead horses, Clark told him, "Oh, those? The vet had to shoot them. They had the glanders." This was Truman's introduction to the man who would one day serve in the U.S. Senate with him.

The major drive in the Argonne Forest began shortly after midnight on September 26. Truman had ordered his men to eat breakfast before the fighting started and Father Tiernan sat on a tree stump and heard confession. "Then," said Truman, "I stood behind my battery and fired 3,000 rounds of .75 shells from four A.M. to eight A.M. and then went forward for more trouble than I was in ever before."

This was one of the war's cruelest fighting zones with all the nastiness of trench warfare. No man's land was pitted with shell craters and mile after mile of barbed-wire entanglement. Truman won a reputation here both for personal bravery and his narrow escapes. Once he and Major Gates, his battalion commander, went forward alone and machine-gun fire pinned them in a ditch for hours. His men had given him up for dead when Truman suddenly reappeared and ordered the battery to follow him across the dismal no man's land. Another night he was sleeping at the edge of a grove of trees. He roused himself and had just walked away when a German shell exploded directly on the spot where he had been resting. Another time a rear French 155 battery fired a burst of shells that just cleared the top of his head. Had he been six feet tall instead of five feet ten inches in height, he would have been killed. Still another close shave came on the night of September 28, while he was directing fire between the towns of Chépy and Varennes. He was riding his horse and low-hanging branches swept his glasses off his face. At his sudden almost complete loss of sight, he turned about desperately. There just in back of the saddle, moonlight shone on the glasses.

Dizzy D reached its glory one night when Truman was reconnoitering far in front of the American line, in order to spot the enemy's positions. His purpose was to report back firing data to his own gun crews situated in an apple orchard, so they would know where to direct their fire. He was under strict orders to fire only at German batteries facing the 35th Division, for to prevent confusion the High Command had given each division a corridor of action.

However, when the skies lighted up with bursting shells, he spied a large German force moving stealthily around the flank of the 35th. Soon it would be upon the 28th Division, next to the 35th, which was not aware that it might soon be overrun. There was no time to report this news back to headquarters, so he violated orders by instructing his own gun crews to fire outside their sector.

The result was that one German battery was destroyed, two others knocked out of commission and the secret attack halted. "How many of the men of the infantry," wrote the regimental historian, "digging in on the open hillsides overhanging Charpentry and Baulny, owe their lives to the alertness, initiative and efficiency of Captain Truman." Yet for a time afterward, Colonel Klemm threatened him with court-martial.

During this bitter fighting, gunsmoke fouled the air, vermin infested the trenches and the men were unshaven, tired and dirty. Occasionally Lieutenant Harry Vaughan, commanding Battery D of the 130th Field Artillery, saw Truman at the front. He was always surprised at Truman's appearance. "Dirt and cooties didn't seem to stick to him the way they did to the rest of us. Harry Truman hadn't had his clothes off his back for two weeks and yet he was immaculate. Moreover, he was clean-shaven. He must have shaved with coffee because we didn't have plain hot water."

On October 3, Truman's division fell into position facing Verdun on the Meuse River. Pershing's objective was to capture Sedan, also on the river, where the French had met humiliating defeat in the War of 1870 against the Germans. With the fall of Sedan now, the entire Hindenburg Line was bound to collapse, bringing with it the end of the war. The hills in the Sommedieu sector, where the 129th operated, were crowded with German machine-gunners and the muddy terrain was dangerous.

Truman's men were sent hedge-hopping from one front line to another all that month. At the beginning of November, Battery D was firing barrages at Metz. Then Sedan fell on the sixth and the German Army collapsed. But the war continued until eleven A.M. on November 11. "It was so quiet it made your head ache," Truman said after the Armistice began. Before the quiet of Armistice Day, more than 100,000 American boys had lost their lives.

Battery D did not leave for home until April 1919. The Prince of Wales came once to review the 129th in a heavy downpour at Courcemont. Another time Truman went to Paris to watch President Wilson as he rode down the boulevard on a December day. The immense crowds were cheering, "Vive Wilson! Vive les États-Unis!" The hope of humanity to make the world safe for democracy was centered on the bespectacled man tipping his hat to the crowd along the Champs-Élysées. It was an emotional sight Truman would never forget.

On April 9, Truman boarded the captured German passenger liner, *Zeppelin,* for the return voyage to civilian life. As his train later pulled out of New York and clicked across the country to Missouri, he had ample time to consider what his war experiences meant to him. It was only a year that he had been away from the United States, yet it seemed like a century. He had left the farmer behind him and was returning home with a broader outlook on the meaning of life and with a surer opinion of his own capabilities to lead men. "I've always been sorry I did not get a university education in the regular way," he said later. "But I got it in the Army the hard way—and it stuck."

6

***

TRUMAN & JACOBSON, HABERDASHERS

In May 1919, Truman was discharged from the Army as a major at Camp Funston, Kansas, and he and Bess Wallace were married on June 28. The wedding took place at Trinity Episcopal Church in Independence, with Ted Marks, a former captain of Battery C, serving as Truman's best man. The boys of Battery Dizzy D had been invited and they provided the only mistake. Instead of going to Bess's church, they proceeded to the Baptist church, since Truman was a Baptist. A wedding was also taking place there and it was not until they saw the groom that they realized their error. However, a quick dash to Trinity Episcopal Church corrected this situation.

After a short honeymoon trip to Chicago and Detroit, the Trumans returned to Independence. Instead of renting or buying a home of their own, they moved into the Gates house at 219 North Delaware with Bess's mother and her grandmother, Elizabeth Emery Gates. Grandfather George Gates had passed away in 1918.

The Gates house was certainly a fancier place than Truman could have rented or purchased at the time. Despite the fifty-five years it had already stood, the house was in superb condition. Among its fourteen high-ceilinged rooms were seven bedrooms, three marble-manteled fireplaces, a large parlor, music room, a dining room that could accommodate thirty at dinner and a long porch at the rear of the house where Sunday supper was customarily taken. Some of the windows had stained glass borders and the house was filled with an exacting collection of antique furniture.

With his housing problem settled there remained the need for earning a livelihood. Truman had no intention to return to farming, and as for his old oil business, he met with Dave Morgan, his partner, and they agreed to dissolve the firm.

He was in Kansas City considering business opportunities early in July when he ran into Eddie Jacobson, his helper at the regimental canteen at Camp Doniphan. Eddie had sold shirts before the war and he mentioned to Truman that he hoped he could improve himself rather than resume his trade as a traveling salesman. "Maybe we ought to go into business together and have our partnership again," Truman said, while they talked about their canteen and its success.

On the spot they decided to open a sort of civilian canteen, a men's furnishings store. Jacobson would do the buying, Truman would handle the books and the two would do the selling. They shook hands on the deal and went off to raise the necessary money to open a store.

Truman sold the stock and equipment on the Grandview farm, and for this $20,000 gave his mother, brother and sister a quitclaim on his quarter-share interest in the farm. He spent $5,000 buying a Kansas City flat, which he rented for income, and put the remaining $15,000 into his partnership with Jacobson, who raised a similar amount.

Truman & Jacobson opened for business at 104 West Twelfth Street in downtown Kansas City on November 29, 1919, with a shelf stock of $35,000 worth of men's furnishings. Truman, who was past thirty-five now, realized he was making a late start in business and hoped he had taken the right step. But he reassured himself with the reminder that a postwar boom was on.

"We opened the store at eight o'clock in the morning and closed at nine at night," Jacobson said. "Twelfth Street was in its heyday and our war buddies and the Twelfth Street boys and girls were our customers. Those were the days when the boys wore silk underwear and silk shirts. We sold silk shirts at $16. Our business was all cash. No credit. Harry and I worked reverse shifts and we had a clerk all the time."

The men of Dizzy D made the store their headquarters. They came in to buy ties and socks and belts and stayed to swap war memories. They liked to linger near the center cabinet in the store where Truman had set the silver loving cup they had given him—TO CAPTAIN HARRY FROM BATTERY D. Jacobson recalled that "Truman was their financial adviser, legal adviser and everything else." They acted toward Truman as though he were their father and involved him in all their personal problems. "I used to drive the boys who hung around the store pretty hard, especially the Catholics," he said. "I used to make them go to Mass."

He encouraged many of his former battery mates to go on to college. One whom he prodded was Albert Ridge, a Battery D private who enrolled at law school and studied in the store. "We had a balcony up over the store," said Truman, "and I used to send him up there to work on his books at night." Jacobson added, "Ridge liked to talk, but Harry would make him get busy and study. Harry really kept Al's nose to the grindstone." Truman also tried to broaden Ridge's reading by suggesting books, such as Plutarch's *Lives,* Franklin's *Autobiography,* Shakespeare, the Bible and Plato's *Republic.* Ridge later became a federal judge.

Business far surpassed expectations that first year. The partners sold more than $70,000 worth of goods and with bright visions of the future plowed their earnings back into the business buying large quantities of goods. They were on a six-day-a-week basis and Truman seldom got home before midnight. On Sundays, he took his wife to Grandview to visit his mother. There the grand old lady sat in her rocking chair while Truman and his sister Mary Jane played classical duets on the upright piano. Then it was back to Twelfth Street for another busy week.

In January 1921, the store's inventory was valued at $35,-000. One man came in and offered to buy them out at a profit, but the partners rejected the offer. Yet only a few months passed before they were sorry.

Shortly after President Warren Harding took the oath of office on March 4, the postwar economic bubble burst. The high government spending during the war had created jobs and increased incomes. Even after the government stopped its heavy purchasing, prosperity continued for a while. But now the civilian economy settled back and a short postwar depression began. Farm prices fell drastically. Then like a chain reaction, prices of manufactured goods began dropping as buyers grew scarce and unemployment common.

Unfortunately, Truman and Jacobson had stocked their

shelves with goods bought before the prices fell. To meet competition they had to slash selling prices until their profit margin vanished. Even so, there were few buyers.

Business was in the doldrums except for the fall of 1921 when the American Legion descended on Kansas City for its national convention. Truman was one of the first to join the Legion as well as being the founder and president of the first Officers Reserve Corps. The result was that Legionnaires poured into the store to buy from their war buddy and relive those hard battles in France. Harry Vaughan was one who came in to see Truman. Vaughan had graduated from Westminster College, a Presbyterian institution at Fulton, Missouri, and was now a chemical engineer.

But the Legion was now gone after days of childish hi-jinks and horseplay, and business disappeared with its departure. While he waited for business to pick up, Truman did a great deal of reading at the counter. Jacobson remembered that he read several books about Andrew Jackson. He also remembered the sad lot of war veterans who lost their jobs and wandered into the store. "Instead of buying," he said, "the boys came in for loans. When they came in asking for Captain Harry, I knew it was for a touch. But if they asked for Captain Truman then I knew we had a sale."

At the beginning of 1922, the previous year's $35,000 inventory was worth only $10,000, and much of what they had was not paid for. When suppliers demanded payment, the partners borrowed $2,500 from the Twelfth Street Bank in January to meet part of their debts. Truman had sold his Kansas City flat the previous year and had used the $5,000 as a down payment on a 160-acre farm costing $13,800 in Johnson County, Kansas. When more creditors demanded payment, he put up the farm as security on a $5,000 loan from the Security State Bank.

The day arrived when their creditors demanded further payments and they were unable to borrow additional money from the bank. This was happening throughout the country to hundreds of thousands of small businessmen, who found a solution by going to court and being declared legal bankrupts. Thus they could wipe out their slate of debts and be absolved from paying their bills.

This simple solution displeased Truman and Jacobson, for they did not want the stigma of being known as bankrupt merchants. Instead, Truman wrote to each creditor and explained the situation. He asked that they take back the remaining stock, deduct their value from the outstanding bills and agree to payment in time on the remaining debt balance.

When the creditors happily agreed, the partners returned their stock and then closed their business. Truman figured that the experience had cost him about $30,000, including the $15,000 he originally put into the business.

But the two men were still not out of the woods. There remained $1,000 owed to suppliers and the two bank loans totaling $7,500. A further harsh stroke befell them when their former landlord insisted that they had to pay him $3,900 for the three years left on their five-year lease.

By the end of 1924, Truman and Jacobson had repaid the $2,500 Twelfth Street Bank loan, sent small sums to suppliers and given Security State $1,200 on its $5,000 loan. However, interest so far on the $5,000 loan amounted to $1,800. So instead of reducing that debt, the former partners found that they now owed Security State $5,600!

Jacobson had returned to the road as a shirt salesman. By February 1925, he could no longer stand the pressure of the

headed the most powerful Democratic machine in Kansas City, the urban center of the county.

It was during a conversation with Jim Pendergast that Truman confided his ambition to run for county judge in the Eastern District of Jackson County. Jackson County elected three county commissioners, or county judges, as they were called, despite the fact that they did not preside over a regular court. The rural part of Jackson County elected the Eastern judge; Kansas City proper, the Western Jackson County judge; and the entire county voted for a presiding judge. The duties of the three judges included levying and collecting local taxes, caring for roads and county buildings and managing the homes for the aged and delinquent children.

Although Jim told his father that Truman would be an admirable candidate for judge, Truman realized he would have to exert additional pressure on Mike Pendergast before he could gain his approval. So one morning he paid a call on Colonel William M. Southern, editor of the Independence *Examiner* and an influential man in local Democratic politics.

Southern said that Truman walked in and bluntly asked, "Colonel, who are the Pendergast and Shannon bosses whom I need to see in Independence if I am going to run for office?" Joseph Shannon ran the other major Democratic machine in the county in competition with the Pendergasts and it was then impossible for any Democratic candidate to win office without the backing of either machine.

"Harry, what in blazes are you talking about?" Southern demanded.

"I mean to run for county judge from the Eastern District."

"Look, Harry," Southern said, "I know you're discouraged

over your business failure and I'm sorry. But don't mess up your whole life by going into politics. It's no disgrace to have failed in business. Many good men have done that. You'll make good at some other business."

Southern later reported that he abused Truman "like a pickpocket for an hour. I told him all the bad effects a life of chronic campaigning could have on a man. I told him how poor were its rewards, how the constant need for popular approval could undermine a man's character. I told him how hard it was on a man's family to have him in politics. Still he smiled and shook his head and repeated he intended to make a career in politics."

Yet afterward, Colonel Southern passed word on to the Pendergast machine that Truman was the man to nominate. And not many days later Mike Pendergast stopped his car in front of the haberdashery store. Truman recalled that he was "standing behind the counter feeling fairly blue when Pendergast entered. He didn't know I was busted."

"How would you like to be county judge?" Mike asked him.

"I don't know," was Truman's hesitant but shrewd reply.

"If you would, you can have it," Mike said.

In June, Mike called a meeting of his Democratic Club at his headquarters, and Truman attended. The top local bosses from every township were there when Mike announced, "Now I'm going to tell you who you're going to support for county judge."

One man present was already receiving handshakes and murmurs of congratulations when Mike continued, "It's Harry Truman! Harry Truman is a returned soldier, a captain 'over there' with a fine record and whose men didn't want to shoot him!"

The man who had been receiving handshakes fell limply in his seat and cheers went up for Truman.

Even with Mike Pendergast's backing, it was necessary for Truman to run in the Democratic primary, and running against him were four other candidates. Unknown to Truman, and even to Mike Pendergast at the time, was that Tom Pendergast, the top boss of the machine, had made a deal with the competing Shannon machine. Joe Shannon had agreed to swing his machine behind Tom Pendergast's candidate for Western District judge in exchange for Pendergast support of Shannon's man for the Eastern District judgeship. This meant that both machines were pledged to support Truman's opponent, Emmett Montgomery, a rich banker from Blue Springs.

Even if Truman had known about this deal he would not have quit the race, for his middle initial could have stood for "Spunky," the quality of a fighter who gave battle without let-up. When he started his campaign, he was short of money and the best campaign vehicle he could afford was a battered old Dodge roadster. The roads were so bad that he had to pile bags of cement into the jalopy to keep from being thrown through the windshield as he bounced along from town to town. He set for himself a rigorous schedule that called for dozens of speeches at picnics and political gatherings as well as a thorough house-to-house canvass of the seven townships in the district.

The Shannon machine expressed great shock that his candidacy had been permitted and set out to destroy him before he could make any headway. Montgomery checked into Truman's record and was overjoyed to discover that he had supported a Republican for county marshal in 1920. This support of Major John Miles, the Shannon machine charged, proved conclusively that Truman was not a Democrat.

This issue came up at Truman's first speech at Oak Grove. With emotion, Truman demolished the issue and turned it to his advantage. "You have heard it said that I voted for John Miles for county marshal," he said. "I'll have to plead guilty to that charge, along with some five thousand ex-soldiers. I was closer to John Miles than a brother. I have seen him hold the American line when only John Miles and his three batteries were between the Germans and a successful counterattack. He was of the right stuff, and a man who wouldn't vote for his comrade under circumstances such as these would be untrue to his country. I have no apology to make."

As the campaign moved along, Truman grew optimistic. He believed he could count on the support of his wartime buddies, his Masonic brothers and many of the farmers he had known during his ten years on the Young farm. At that time the Ku Klux Klan, the force of racial and religious bigotry, was sweeping the nation. The white-robed and hooded gangs were burning their fiery crosses on the property of those who opposed them. In Jackson County, they operated openly and claimed majority support.

By instinct and principle, Truman opposed the KKK. But many of the veterans who backed him were members and insisted that he join if he wanted to win the primary. Against his own better judgment, Truman reluctantly agreed to become a member in name only. The day came when he had to appear for his initiation at the Baltimore Hotel in Kansas City. With great distaste he showed up at the gathering, and in the midst of this sea of hate, the Grand Kleagle of the local

Klan said to him, "You've got to promise us that you won't give a Catholic a job if you belong to us."

Truman's face grew brick-red with anger. "I won't agree to anything like that," he exploded. "I had a Catholic battery in the war and if any of those boys need help, I'm going to give them jobs."

"Get out of here!" the Grand Kleagle told him.

The KKK now became his enemy, but Truman didn't care. In fact, he later helped organize a group that ran the Klan's leaders out of the county.

Primary Day fell on August first. Early election returns showed Truman running neck and neck with Montgomery. However, late that afternoon word reached Truman headquarters that Shannon's men planned to steal the ballot box at Mt. Washington and stuff it with sufficient ballots to ensure Montgomery's victory. Judge Henry Bundschu related what followed:

"John Miles, the county marshal, sent his brother George and a young soldier, John Gibson, out to the precinct to preserve peace. They had not been there long before three or four taxicabs pulled up in the street and a lot of tough fellows emerged. Gibson said he became scared, but reached in his holster and pulled out his .45-caliber revolver. He cocked it and stuck it into the stomach of the man nearest him. He said the man turned pale, raised his hand and said, 'Come on, boys, let's go!' After that, things quieted down, and the judges and clerks counted the ballots." The man young Gibson frightened was Joe Shannon, the leader of the powerful county Democratic machine.

When the vote was finally tallied, the result showed Truman the victor over Montgomery by fewer than 500 votes. But those votes were sufficient to give him his start in politics.

8

JUDGE TRUMAN OF JACKSON COUNTY

By the time Truman took the oath of office in January 1923, he had already mapped out for himself an ambitious political future. Of course, he did not discuss this publicly at the time, for to have done so would have made him into a laughingstock. As a raw beginner in politics, he would have sounded ridiculous had he disclosed his desire to become presiding judge of the three-man county court after a term or two as Jackson County Eastern District judge. Following this, he hoped to go to Washington as a member of the House of Representatives, then to Jefferson City as Governor of Missouri and finally to the United States Senate—his final objective.

For the time being, however, he had to make good as a county judge, and this he set out to do. He had first to meet the animosity of Joe Shannon, who seethed at what he believed was a doublecross and sarcastically declared that "the voters preferred a busted merchant to a prosperous banker." Shannon's man had won the office of presiding county judge, but he lacked any authority because Truman and Henry F. McElroy, the Western District judge, consistently outvoted him. The result was that Shannon let word get out that he would end Truman's short political career at the next election.

Truman had another problem in fellow judge McElroy, a corrupt politician whose chief purpose was to perform profitable favors for the Pendergast machine. McElroy considered Truman a strange sort because he talked about public service and the public trust. Jackson County was a unique county insofar as it maintained two county courthouses, one in Kansas City and the other in Independence, with the county seat in Independence. At the outset, McElroy attempted to browbeat Truman into agreeing to a transfer of the county seat to Kansas City. This would have placed the county directly under the thumb of Tom Pendergast, the big boss. Truman refused to agree to this historic loss for Independence and McElroy told a reporter, "I tried to get it moved. But a lot of little fellows around Independence Square made such a howl that the move failed."

Nevertheless, Truman did manage to cooperate with McElroy on some matters, even though they disagreed on principles. For instance, in 1919, the state legislature had given control of county institutions to circuit judges who were regular case-trying judges. Truman considered this a violation of the state constitution, which had established such control in the hands of the county judges; McElroy wanted the resumption of county control because it would mean more jobs and lucrative contracts for the Pendergast machine. So the two cooperated and won a favorable decision from the state supreme court.

The last county court had run the county into debt by more than a million dollars. Much of this had gone for graft to road overseers who paid themselves large sums of money for hundreds of culverts that were never built and for road repairs that were never made. Other large sums had been paid out for high-quality concrete when thin, low-grade cement was used instead and for fictitious expenditures to operate the old-age and juvenile county homes.

Quietly, Truman began a close check on county expenditures and despite objections from the Pendergast machine he made deep inroads into economy and better service. Just how well he succeeded can be seen from an editorial in the Kansas City *Star,* a bitter opponent of the Pendergast machine. In its August 3, 1924, issue, the *Star* told readers: "The present county court is busy paying off the debt. It paid off more than $600,000 last year. It has improved the roads. It has money in the treasury. This is the difference between county courts." The paper went on to promote Truman and McElroy for a second term.

Although Truman worked hard at his job, he still found time for other activities. For a better understanding of the legal technicalities involved in his work, he enrolled in evening classes at the Kansas City Law School. Dean Edward D. Ellison said he was a good student, considering that he had full-time responsibilities elsewhere. "Truman attended the academic years of 1923–1924 and 1924–1925," said Ellison. "He made a general average of B in the subjects he took." Truman also joined the Kansas City Athletic Club and at the age of forty finally learned to swim. He used an unorthodox side stroke, keeping his head out of the water because he wore glasses while swimming. Some time went to activities in the 59th Masonic District of Jackson County, where by 1924 he rose to Deputy Grand Master. Generally, he spent Sundays visiting his mother, and still played duets with Mary Jane on the old upright piano.

During this period he had also resumed National Guard training, and each summer attended maneuvers at Camp Riley, Kansas. He came one time to Camp Riley sporting a bristle mustache. Another time he tried to raise a beard, but he shaved it off because "the hair on the right side of my face grew upward and on the left side it grew down." It was at the summer encampments that he ran into Harry Vaughan, from Camp Doniphan days, and John Snyder, who had attended artillery school with him at Coetquidan. Truman was now a lieutenant colonel commanding the 379th Regiment and Captains Vaughan and Snyder headed the 380th and 381st. Vaughan was then a salesman for a railroad tie company and Snyder worked in a bank. There was also a fourth member of this close group, Edward E. McKim, who had been a sergeant in Battery D and was now a lieutenant.

So far as Truman was concerned the most important event during his term as county judge came on February 17, 1924, when his daughter, Mary Margaret Truman, was born. Bess Truman's grandmother, eighty-three-year-old Elizabeth Gates, was overjoyed because this brought four generations under the same roof. As for Truman, he was so excited that he forgot to buy a crib, and for a short time Margaret had to be bedded down in a dresser drawer.

When baby Margaret was only a few months old, Truman had to run for renomination in the Democratic primary. Joe Shannon had been waiting for this opportunity to take care of the political upstart, as he called Truman, and he selected a man highly regarded in the county to oppose him. Shannon also lined up the Ku Klux Klan against him, even though Shannon was a Roman Catholic.

The Kansas City *Star* reported that "great feeling was aroused over this race." Nevertheless, Truman was an easy victor, infuriating Shannon still further. There was still the general election coming up in November, and Shannon decided to deliver his machine to the Republicans, in order to finish Truman.

By an odd twist of fate, Truman would not have had a Republican opponent in the November election had it not been for his friends. Just before the primary, Major John Miles, Truman's war companion and Republican county marshal, called Henry Bundschu, a circuit court judge and also a Truman friend, and told him that no Republican had filed for judge in the Eastern District. Bundschu suggested that Henry Rummell, one of Miles's deputies, file. "Miles agreed," said Bundschu, "with the understanding that Rummell would withdraw as soon as Miles could find some outstanding person qualified for the place. So without saying anything to Rummell about it, I went to the courthouse and filed him for the Republican nomination against Harry Truman."

With no opposition, Rummell won the Republican nomination. Major Miles was chagrined afterward and said, "When I couldn't get any really qualified person to run against Captain Truman, I told Rummell he ought to withdraw. But Rummell said he wasn't going to get out because Joe Shannon was going to support him. It was a dirty thing Henry Bundschu and I did to Harry Truman."

Between the August primary and the November general election, the Shannon machine and the Ku Klux Klan steadily denounced Truman and built up support for Rummell. Rummell was an elderly man whom Truman remembered from his childhood as the person who made a set of harnesses so that he and his little brother Vivian could hitch their goats to a small wagon.

As the November election approached, the Ku Kluxers spoke openly of harming Truman physically. "They threatened to kill me," he said. "And I went out to one of their meetings and dared them to try. I poured it into them. Then I came down from the platform and walked through them to my car." Just as he got behind the wheel, several of his friends drove up, armed with shotguns. "It was a good thing they did not come earlier," Truman added. "If they had, there would have been trouble."

However, Truman's personal bravery did not help him in the election. The combination of the Shannon machine, the KKK and the Republican organization proved overwhelming and Rummell defeated him by 867 votes. Rummell became a celebrity of sorts years afterward because he could claim to have been the only man to defeat Truman in an election contest.

9

JACKSON COUNTY'S
PRESIDING JUDGE

AT THE TIME Truman retired to private life in January 1925, the country was in the midst of the Coolidge-era prosperity. But, as he admitted, "I was broke and out of a job." In February, Eddie Jacobson had filed his petition in bankruptcy and not long afterward Truman quit law school to concentrate on earning a livelihood for his family.

The first job Truman took was to sell memberships in the Kansas City Automobile Club. Within a year he sold more than a thousand memberships, earning $5,000, or $2,000 more than his previous salary as county judge. There were several other opportunities that came along during this time. The president of the Security State Bank of Englewood was willing to sell his bank to Truman and two friends for $30,-000. When he agreed to settle the deal without requiring a down payment, the three became bankers. However, Truman did not remain here long because in checking the books, he found that the previous owner had fraudulently misused the bank's deposits. After reporting the true situation to the bonding company, he withdrew from the firm.

In 1925, Truman also organized the Community Savings and Loan Association in Independence and became its president. This turned out successfully, but he found he lacked the same high interest in business that he had in public life. When he learned that the National Old Trails Association was seeking a new president, he made application and got the job. The N.O.T.A. was a national organization devoted to building excellent highways over the famous pioneer trails that had shaped American history in the nineteenth century.

"I was president of the first transcontinental idea of a road from Baltimore to Los Angeles," he said. "Fort Cumberland was the first milestone on the Old National Road and I helped lay it out—me and Henry Clay."

Truman's job with the N.O.T.A. required a great deal of traveling and speaking. Little Margaret remembered afterward the numerous trips she took with her parents when her father inspected the old trails and laid out highways. From his childhood readings, he knew in great detail the fascinating history of the old Boston Post Road, Braddock Road, Cumberland Road, the National Pike, the Santa Fe and Oregon Trails and he relived their awesome glories as he sped about the country. Once he came to Washington and addressed the Daughters of the American Revolution to win their support for his work. Another time he led an N.O.T.A. delegation to Kansas for a conference with the governor. When he returned home, he went to Grandview to tell his mother about his meeting with the governor. She heard him out and then asked him, "You didn't by any chance spy my mother's silver that Jim Lane's Red-Legs stole back in sixty-one?"

In the late spring of 1926, Bess Truman caught sight of her husband's restlessness as the time for the Democratic primaries approached. He began talking to her at home about running for office again. There was one county office that was high in salary but low in prestige and he desired it, if only to clear up the debts from the haberdashery store and provide a nest egg for his family. "I wanted to be county collector, which carried an unusual remuneration of $25,000 a year in salaries and fees," he said. This was more than eight times the salary of a county judge.

There was, however, a high hurdle to leap over if he were to win this nomination. Without the expressed support of Tom Pendergast, whose Democratic organization now completely dominated Kansas City and the rest of Jackson County, he did not stand a ghost of a chance. He could either come hat in hand to Tom Pendergast and ask for his support or he could forget about reentering politics. Faced with these alternatives, he decided to call on Pendergast, whom he had seen before but had never met.

The Pendergast machine went back to Jim Pendergast, one of nine children of an Irish immigrant who settled in St. Joseph, Missouri. Jim Pendergast, with his permanent smile beneath a thick black mustache on his moon-shaped reddish face, had come to Kansas City in 1876 at the age of twenty. After a short stint as an iron puddler in a foundry, he won a great deal of money betting on a horse named Climax and invested his winnings in a saloon and a "barrel house," a combination rooming house and restaurant. He was such a genial man and so free with handouts to the many poor people in Kansas City's First Ward that in 1892 they voted him their alderman in the city council.

After this, Jim Pendergast created a political machine that proved strong enough to elect a mayor in 1900. To help him run his machine, he brought brothers Mike and Tom to Kansas City. Mike did not reveal sufficient leadership qualities to serve as Jim's chief aide, and in time he was allotted one ward in town and the rural part of the county as his territory.

But Tom Pendergast proved a natural for machine politics. He wore a black derby on his almost bald head and owned a deep bass voice that could cut through a roomful of loud talkers. He was not tall, but his weightlifter's torso, enormous face and hamlike hands made him appear bigger. His eyes were a searing hypnotic gray and easily saw through the schemes and ambitions of friend and foe. Once he was aroused, he had a ferocious temper and took direct action with his fists. Tom's fistic talents were well known, especially his achievement at knocking "Fireman" Jim Flynn unconscious in a barroom brawl. Flynn was the only boxer who knocked out Jack Dempsey in a prize fight.

Tom started out in politics as deputy constable in the First Ward, moving up to precinct captain and superintendent of streets as he gained experience. His work in the precincts was especially important, for he learned not only the habits of each citizen at this lowest political level but also what was needed to keep the voters on his brother's side. He learned that voters would support the machine in exchange for favors such as a free bushel of soft coal, a job, an operation. Every Christmas there was a free turkey dinner for the poor and toys for the kiddies. And Tom would be there, his head so large it resembled a pumpkin on a tree stump, as he reminded the diners that the Pendergasts were paying the bill.

Machines, both Democratic and Republican, were commonplace in every American city, and the Pendergast machine in Kansas City was, therefore, not unique. They were simply a scheme by a handful of men to gain political control in the various metropolises and channel the cities' spending into their own pockets. Handouts to the poor were a cheap but necessary expenditure in the process of enriching themselves.

When brother Jim died in 1911, Tom Pendergast took over the machine. He was aware that his own personal fortune depended on his continuing political power. With his henchmen holding office, he was assured that they would award highly profitable contracts to the road and building construction companies he owned or controlled. In addition, he was president of the Ready Mixed Concrete Company and city inspectors rejected all jobs that did not use his concrete. He also controlled the firm that hauled away the garbage of Kansas City. His opponents found that for weeks on end garbage pick-up trucks would forget to stop at their houses. Tom Pendergast did not drink but he owned a wholesale liquor firm. Saloons in town had to serve his whisky or lose their licenses. Citizens who openly provoked him learned to their sorrow that the tax rates on their businesses and homes had been increased so steeply that they could no longer afford to maintain stores or residences.

For a long time Tom Pendergast was not secure. Besides the Republican machines in Kansas City that were busy in the same business, he had an arch Democratic rival in the person of Joe Shannon. To distinguish between the two Democratic machines, local citizens called the Pendergast faction "Goats" and the Shannons, "Rabbits." A reporter originated the nicknames with a story in which he wrote: "The Pendergast crowd voted everything in sight, even the goats on the hillside. The Shannon forces flock to the polls like scared rabbits after the hunter has beaten the bush."

By 1926, when Harry Truman decided to return to politics, the Pendergast Goats had decisively wrested control of the county's Democrats from Shannon's Rabbits. More than that, Tom Pendergast was now undisputed boss of Jackson County. Henry McElroy, who had served with Truman as a county judge, was now the city manager of Kansas City and for the next thirteen years he and Tom Pendergast were to dictate the affairs of that city. As McElroy baldly put it, "Tom and I are partners. He takes care of politics and I take care of the business. Every Sunday morning, at Tom's house or mine, we meet and talk over what's best for the city."

To Pendergast, taking care of politics meant controlling the individual voter. "We fill his belly, warm his back and vote him our way," he explained his method. "You've got to have boss leadership," he tried to justify his undemocratic political power. "Now look at me. I'm not bragging when I say I run the show in Kansas City. I am boss. If I was a Republican they would call me 'leader.' "

Tom Pendergast owned a home that cost him $150,000 and its interior decorations several hundred thousand dollars more. One time when a burglar ransacked his house, his daughter Marceline reported that among her losses were 480 pairs of silk stockings. Yet Pendergast's political headquarters consisted of a squalid three-room suite filled with secondhand furniture above a fried-food cafe at 1908 Main Street in the shabbier business area of Kansas City. He could be found here from six A.M. until noon, when he left through his secret exit to go to the race track and to handle his various business enterprises. During his political hours, his waiting room's little, hard chairs were crowded with politicians, beggars, contractors, job seekers and anyone else who wanted a word with the big boss. His waiting room was governed by a muscular, husky, former river boat captain named Elijah Matheus. "Cap" Matheus had strict orders to send visitors into Pendergast's inner office on a first come, first serve basis, without regard to rank.

It was to this yellowish-brick building and up the worn, creaking stairs that Harry Truman had to come if he wanted to resume his political career. He was not alone in this endeavor, for governors, judges and Congressmen were also forced to make this same trip.

After Truman waited a while in the outer office, "Cap" Matheus ushered him into the boss's small, barren office and there he found Tom Pendergast in his swivel chair behind a splintered roll-top desk, his hat jammed on his head and a look of impatience on his face. To Truman's request for the machine's support to back him for county collector, Pendergast let out a decisive, "No!"

Tom Pendergast said he had already promised the job to someone else, but he assured his disappointed visitor that the Goats would be glad to back him for presiding judge of the county court. Of course, this paid only $3,000 a year, compared with the $25,000 for county collector. Truman could take it or leave it.

Mike Pendergast was angry when he heard what his younger brother had offered Truman. He insisted that Truman run for county collector and disregard Tom. But Truman realized that the machine belonged to Tom and not to Mike Pendergast, and without Tom's support he had no future. So after discussing the situation with his wife, Truman ran for presiding judge.

Truman had no Shannon Rabbit opponent in the Democratic primary, though Joe Shannon spoke disparagingly at every opportunity. "Harry Truman has the habit of dancing around nervously," he said one time. "The fellow's always grinning and he's too quick with his mouth. He talks off the cuff at the wrong time."

In the November 1926 general election, Truman defeated his Republican opponent by 16,000 votes. He had traveled throughout the county repeating at gathering after gathering his intention of providing the county with honest and economic government. To many political insiders this was good for a horselaugh and a wink because they knew from past experience that Goat officeholders were beholden to Tom Pendergast's orders. Moreover, they were aware that Pendergast had agreed to give Shannon some of the spoils as well as the right to a third of the political jobs in rural Jackson County.

Truman's trial by fire came only days after he was sworn into office in January 1927, when Pendergast telephoned him and suggested he join him in a meeting with Shannon. Truman was well aware what was at stake because, as he recounted, "the court appointed the purchasing agent, county welfare officers, a county auditor, heads of homes, approved the budget of elected officials, such as treasurer, county clerk, circuit clerk, county collector, county assessor, county highway engineer." Involved were 900 jobs and a budget that ran into the millions.

When he came to the meeting, Tom Pendergast met him in the outer office. "Now look here, Harry," he warned him, "they tell me you're a pretty hotheaded fellow. But I want you to understand that when we are in this meeting I don't want any fighting."

The three men sat around the table: the powerful boss, the faded boss and the Goat officeholder. "There are three sides to any question," Pendergast told Shannon. "Your side, my side and the right side."

Truman said nothing while the two bosses began an argument over political spoils. They pounded on the table, called each other names and finally Pendergast half-rose and cocked a fist, prepared to smash it into Shannon's face. Suddenly he glanced at Truman, who had been watching this primitive show with a broad grin on his face. His grin did something to Pendergast, for he fell back in his seat and grinned, too.

The meeting ended with no lucrative rewards for Shannon. "Let the river take its course," Pendergast said vaguely. Afterward, when Shannon was gone, Pendergast had a talk with Truman. "You will have to put my friends into the key jobs," he told him. "But if you are not satisfied with their work, go ahead and fire them and appoint your own men."

On this note, Truman began his eight years of service as Jackson County's presiding judge.

10

ROAD MAKER AND
COURTHOUSE BUILDER

JUDGE TRUMAN proved to be a controversial Goat from the very beginning. He accepted Pendergast's suggested appointees, but not many weeks went by before he "fired people left and right who didn't work in the county's interest." He also inaugurated an inspection and auditing system "which gave the crooked contractors an awful pain." Then, he admitted proudly, "I stopped the expense account system of road overseers and cut the number of these overseers from sixty to sixteen. That was an unpopular move because it isn't good politics in any party to reduce the number of jobs, and I was as unpopular as a skunk in the parlor."

"Judge Truman threw the organization into an uproar," said a Pendergast lieutenant. "They weren't accustomed to anyone acting on his own. Any day they expected old Tom to squelch Harry. But he never lifted a finger."

Truman felt a compulsion to solve the mammoth problems of the county. "When I took over as the executive officer of the county," he explained, "I found its road system a wreck, its courthouses falling down, its finances in such condition that the state was threatening to send the five or six hundred insane it was caring for back to the county and leave them on the courthouse steps."

For instance, to pay its bills each year before taxes were collected, the county had borrowed money at six percent interest from Goats who owned banks. Since about $2,500,000 was borrowed, the interest involved a substantial sum. When Truman discovered this, he boarded a train to St. Louis and Chicago and bargained with bankers in those cities for tax anticipation loans at lower rates of interest. At first he succeeded in pushing the rate down to four percent and later to two and a half percent.

Truman realized that his major effort must be devoted to doing something about the county's wretched road system. But rather than rely on his own judgment, he appointed a two-man consulting team, one a Democrat and the other a Republican, to conduct an independent survey. When they submitted their report to him in May 1927, what they handed him was a severe indictment of the crooked politics that had saddled the county with almost impassable roads. Their conclusion was that the low quality of the materials used, as well as poorly planned grades and curves, made local transportation dangerous. "There are some 350 miles of what has been aptly termed 'pie-crust' roads," they reported. "The cost of maintaining these roads even in fair condition is almost an impossibility."

They asserted that the only plausible answer was the construction of 224 miles of new roads at a cost of $6,500,000.

Early one morning shortly afterward, Truman climbed the stairs at 1908 Main Street to discuss this with Tom Pendergast. The county lacked ready funds to undertake this work, and only a county issue of bonds guaranteeing future repayment to purchasers would bring in this amount of money.

Pendergast pointed out that City Manager McElroy had prepared a $28,000,000 bond issue for Kansas City that was to be voted on in the spring of 1928. This would pay for a new auditorium, city hall, sewer system, a bridge across the Missouri and a new water plant. If Truman's proposed $6,-500,000 county bond issue came to a vote at the same time, he said, it would endanger the passage of the city bond issue. "Besides," Pendergast added bluntly, "they'll say I'm going to steal it. Every presiding judge for twenty years now has been trying to get a county bond issue without success."

This only served to increase Truman's stubbornness. "I'll tell the people what I mean to do and they'll vote the bonds," he argued.

Pendergast sneered. "Go tell the voters anything you want to."

Someone else would have forgotten about the county bond issue at this point. But since Pendergast had not flatly ruled it out, Truman promptly considered it as a go-ahead signal. When the Kansas City *Star* asserted that he did not have a chance of winning the voters' approval, he grew more intent on its passage.

During the next several months he drove to every hamlet and farm in the county to explain the program and whip up support. He talked about the obvious need for new roads and pledged that a bipartisan board of engineers would run the program. Contracts would go solely to qualified lowest bidders and the political machine would not be permitted to use it to stuff its pockets.

In May 1928 his campaign paid off, for the county bond issue carried by a three-fourths majority, instead of the smaller necessary two-thirds. As for McElroy's Kansas City bond issue, voters rejected all of it except for $250,000.

Truman was well aware that he walked a tightrope by insisting that contracts go to the lowest bidders, since several top Goats were in the contracting business. And trouble was not long in coming.

When he awarded the first road contract for $400,000 to a South Dakota firm, his phone rang almost immediately. It was Tom Pendergast suggesting that he come to a meeting in his office with several local Goat contractors.

The three leading "pie-crust" road builders were at that session, and they immediately pitched into Truman in an effort to force him to rescind his first contract. "Bill Ross was the spokesman for the trio," said Truman, "and he demanded that the contracts go to local bidders. They gave me the old song and dance about being local citizens and taxpayers and that they should have an inside track to the construction contracts." But Truman realized that if he permitted them to win contracts his entire program was doomed. "The contracts will have to go to the lowest responsible bidders," he told them flatly.

There was an immediate flare-up and a harsh argument followed. Tom Pendergast said nothing as the three attacked Truman and the bespectacled presiding county judge refused to give in to them. Finally, Pendergast let out a laugh and said to Ross, "I told you, Bill, he's the contrariest man on earth."

"I said I wasn't being contrary," Truman recalled. "I said I was proceeding in a legal and business manner."

Then Pendergast told the contractors, "Get out of here!" When they were gone, he said to Truman, "You carry out your commitments."

After that, the road program proceeded in the manner Truman had promised the voters. N. T. Veatch, the Republican co-administrator of the program, said at its conclusion, "The whole job was as clean as a hound's tooth." The Kansas City *Star* hailed his road-building effort as "extraordinarily honest" with "not a suspicion of graft involved." If there was a chief critic of the road program, it was Truman's mother. He had sliced eleven acres off her property for one of his highway projects and did not pay her for the land he took. She sat in her rocking chair, patted Sinner, her hound dog, and told a reporter, "I'd have gotten eleven thousand dollars if my son wasn't a county judge. If I could have my way, I'd roll up my six hundred acres and move them a hundred miles further from the city. First, our house was a quarter of a mile back from the road. Next, U.S. Highway Number 71 separated the farm into two parts, and finally Blue Ridge Boulevard Extension cut through the maples leading from the house to the Grandview Road."

The popularity of the road program was apparent in 1930, when Judge Truman ran for a second four-year term. This time he won by a majority of 58,000 votes, compared with 16,000 in 1926.

Almost immediately afterward, he promoted a second bond issue for $7,950,000. This time he proposed spending $3,500,000 for additional roads, $500,000 for a new hospital for the aged, $4,000,000 for a new county courthouse in Kansas City and $200,000 to renovate Independence's decrepit county courthouse. This time when he discussed his proposal with Tom Pendergast, the Goat boss accepted it enthusiastically, for he had in mind a large Kansas City bond issue. He saw that the city bond issue might win approval at the polls if it were tied to Truman's county bond proposal. The result was a single $40,000,000 package of both plans, which won by a four to one majority in May 1931.

Of all his new projects, the new county courthouse in Kansas City interested Truman most. The old courthouse was a disgrace with its oil-soaked floors, stale odors and gloomy rooms. He wanted a showplace and he intended to erect one. At his own expense he set out on a 24,000-mile tour of other courthouses throughout the country. He made stops at Brooklyn, Buffalo, Milwaukee, Denver and Houston. The Caddo Parish Courthouse at Shreveport, Louisiana, impressed him most of all and he hired its architect as his consulting engineer.

Truman's final structure was a 22-story building adorned with a statue of Andrew Jackson before its entrance. In his wanderings, he had seen Charles Keck's statue of Jackson at Charlottesville, Virginia, and he employed Keck to portray Jackson astride a horse. Then to be certain of authentic details, Truman journeyed to The Hermitage, Jackson's Tennessee residence, where he personally measured Jackson's actual dress uniform.

In contrast to Truman's program, the Kansas City 10-Year Plan, which resulted from the 1931 bond issue, was taking an opposite turn. City Manager McElroy and Tom Pendergast were using its millions for personal gain. For instance, Kansas City had a little stream named Brush Creek that meandered throughout town. McElroy spent a million dollars paving Brush Creek with Pendergast's Ready Mixed Cement to a depth of eight inches and a width of seventy feet in some areas. Some of the bond money went to keep 6,000 Goats on the city's payroll, many of whom did no work for the city. Investigators later found that McElroy had misused about $11,000,000. During this period also, gangsters infiltrated the political machine in the city and took over some wards.

Some of Truman's friends wondered openly about two questions. The first was why Pendergast tolerated his existence since his operations did not enrich the greedy grafters in the machine. The second question was why Truman did not quit the Goats.

The answer to the first question was that Tom Pendergast needed at least one honest official to help offset the charge that his machine was entirely graft-ridden. The answer to the second question was more complex.

In the summer of 1933, when Colonel Truman attended the National Guard encampment at Camp Pike, Arkansas, Ed Schauffler, a Kansas City reporter, queried him about his connections with Pendergast.

"Tell me, Harry, if you want to," Schauffler asked, "how you, a clean-cut, intelligent public official, with unusually progressive ideas can remain part of a political organization which tolerates the things it does? I'm curious."

Truman smiled and replied, "I don't mind answering at all, Ed. I owe my political life to the Pendergast organization. I never would have had an opportunity to have a career in politics without their support. I know that the organization has countenanced some things which I believe are wrong. But I do believe this, and that is that you can get farther cleaning up a political organization from the inside than you can from the outside."

Actually, Truman was too minor a political figure to clean up the Pendergast machine from the inside. In fact, he had all he could do to protect himself from attacks by the Goat regulars. Nor did Tom Pendergast seek his advice on political or other matters.

The truth was that Pendergast had risen through fortunate circumstances to dominance of the entire state of Missouri and had more important things on his mind than the activities of the rural road builder and courthouse constructor. In 1932, all Missouri candidates for the U.S. House of Representatives had to run for office on a statewide basis and not on the customary basis of individual congressional districts. This was so because the governor had vetoed a bill that determined the area of each congressional district. Because of the importance of the large Kansas City vote, no man could expect to win without Pendergast's support. The result was that Pendergast decided who would go to Congress, as well as who would serve as governor, state supreme court justices, and in other elected state offices. After the 1932 election, Pendergast's office on Main Street became known as the "State Capitol," and the actual Jefferson City State Capitol as "Uncle Tom's Cabin."

By early 1934, Judge Truman had every reason to believe that his political career was drawing to an end. There could be no third term as presiding judge and what efforts he had made to win approval for other posts had met with no success. For example, he said, "When the redistricting of the state for Congress came up in the 1933 legislature, I went to Jefferson City and worked for a congressional district for Eastern Jackson County. I admit that I had in mind the idea of running for Congress from the new district myself. The district was created all right, but Pendergast decided not to support me. So I was out in the cold."

All that faced him was to work hard at his construction projects until his term ended in January 1935, and then disappear from the political scene. Some honors did come his way at this time. He was elected head of a regional organization to plan civic improvements for Missouri and Kansas counties and became a director of the National Conference on City Planning. An editor who attended a conference meeting reported, "Judge Truman far outshone the professors and practitioners present in the discussions on theory and application." In October 1933, he also accepted a dollar-a-year appointment from Federal Emergency Relief Administrator Harry Hopkins as reemployment director of Missouri. The great depression had been going on since 1929 and about 15,000,000 persons throughout the country were unemployed. Truman's task was to find jobs for the unemployed in Missouri in order to prevent starvation. Tom Pendergast disliked President Franklin D. Roosevelt but stood in awe of his financial programs, which made his own seem trifling. "You can't beat five billion dollars," he barked.

Judge Truman celebrated his fiftieth birthday on May 8, 1934. But it was not a day of joy, for he was certain he faced a bleak future.

11

TO THE UNITED STATES SENATE

Dᴜʀɪɴɢ the spring of 1934, while Truman contemplated his grim future, Governor Guy B. Park asked him to take on an extra nonpaying chore. The governor wanted to get a bond issue to rebuild the dilapidated state institutions and he appointed Truman chairman of the bond issue committee because of his success in Jackson County.

Unknown to Truman, while he went out on a speaking tour of thirty-five Missouri counties, Tom Pendergast was in a political predicament. There was to be a contest for a seat in the U.S. Senate that year and he was experiencing difficulty in finding a candidate. His first choice was James A. Reed, whom the machine had installed as mayor in 1900 and then as U.S. Senator from 1910 to 1928, when Reed retired. Reed was best known as a gifted orator and a Democrat who bitterly fought President Woodrow Wilson's proposal for the League of Nations. Reed, however, was seventy-two now and did not want to engage in what promised to be a spirited campaign.

Pendergast then turned to Joe Shannon, his former rival, whom he had sent to the U.S. House of Representatives in 1930 to get him out of the state. Shannon debated whether to accept Pendergast's offer. But after canvassing leading Missouri Democrats, he concluded that a Pendergast choice could not win the Democratic primary.

Pendergast then asked James P. Aylward, Jackson County Democratic Chairman, to run for the Senate. Again he got a refusal and it appeared that he would now be without a candidate.

"I was out speaking for the state bond issue in May 1934," said Truman. "While I was in Warsaw [Missouri], James P. Aylward called me from Sedalia and said he and Jim Pendergast were at the Bothwell Hotel there. They asked me to meet them for a conference."

He was hardly into their Sedalia hotel room when Aylward got to the point of the meeting. Tom Pendergast had decided on Truman for the U.S. Senate. "The organization will back you at least ninety-eight percent," Aylward added.

Although Truman was flattered, he realized that he must have been far down on Pendergast's list of candidates. In addition, he realized that the newspapers were almost unanimously of the opinion that a Pendergast candidate could not win the Democratic nomination, because the gangsters who had infiltrated the machine had turned Kansas City into a place of mammoth crime. Truman told the two Jims that he had no money to make the race and added humbly that he was not well enough known in the state.

It was only after hours of arguing that he finally agreed

to run. On May 14, he wrote in his diary, "It is 4 A.M. I am to make the most momentous decision of my life. I have come to the place where all men strive to be at my age. . . . And now I am a candidate for the United States Senate. If the Almighty God decides that I go there I am going to pray as King Solomon did, for wisdom to do the job."

When he filed for the Senate race, there was great surprise in Kansas City. Said the Kansas City *Star:* "It is agreed Pendergast has taken on a real job. To jump a man from the county court bench to a Senate nomination is quite an undertaking." A friend of Truman's went to see Pendergast and the boss confided: "I don't feel that Harry Truman has a chance."

This was to prove a fierce contest for the Democratic nomination. Bennett Clark, whom Truman had known in France, had delivered a solid defeat to Pendergast in 1932 when he won election to the U.S. Senate. Clark was now contending with Pendergast for control of the state and his man to oppose Truman was Jacob "Tuck" Milligan, who was serving his sixth term in the House of Representatives. Milligan was not Truman's only formidable opponent, for Congressman John J. Cochran of St. Louis had also filed for the primary. Cochran had served in the House since 1926 and had risen to such prominence in Washington that Capitol newsmen had voted him one of the six most useful members of the House.

The Kansas City *Times* reported that "in the whole of Missouri history there have been few such spirited contests within a party."

Truman campaigned vigorously during the four weeks before the August seventh primary. "I went into sixty of Missouri's one hundred and fourteen counties where I made from six to sixteen speeches a day," he said. "I had become acquainted with all the county judges and county clerks in the state of Missouri and was very familiar with the operations of the so-called 'courthouse gangs' in all the country counties. There was a county judge's association with three judges in each. So there was not a precinct in Missouri in which I did not have at least one friend at the polls."

All three candidates and their supporters went after each other in a hard-hitting manner. Truman reminded the voters that while Milligan and Cochran were denouncing him as a Pendergast man, only two years before both men had come hat in hand to Pendergast's upstairs office to plead for support in their congressional contests. He also charged that Senator Clark, as the boss behind Milligan, was trying to establish himself as the boss of Missouri. Clark in turn replied that at Truman's opening speech "the natives looked over the crowd to see if Dillinger was there." Then having attempted to tie in Truman somehow with gangsters, Clark grew wild and called Truman "a common liar" and said his campaign was one of "mendacity and imbecility unparalleled in the history of Missouri."

The withering blows on all sides continued all through July and the St. Louis *Post-Dispatch* denounced the campaign as a case of "the pot, kettle and stewpan calling each other black." Cochran called Milligan the lackey of Clark; and Truman, "Pendergast's office boy." Milligan charged that if Truman became Senator he would get "calluses on his ears listening on the long-distance telephone to his boss." At one point during the month, Truman had "a head-on collision in my car and got a sprained wrist and some broken ribs." But even though he was temporarily incapacitated, his followers continued the word battle.

Why this strange campaign? The answer was simple. All three Democrats believed in President Roosevelt's New Deal and were in complete agreement on political issues. This left them with nothing to debate except the personal integrity of their opponents.

Newspapermen believed that Truman would be badly defeated by his opponents, and when early returns came they bore out this prediction. Close to midnight, Cochran led with 234,580, Truman was second with 139,321 and Milligan trailed with 138,702. Then came the late returns and Truman picked up 137,529 votes; Cochran only 1,525 more; and Milligan, 8,912. Truman had come through with a plurality of about 40,000 votes.

The day after the primary, the Kansas City *Star* announced: "Tom Pendergast today stands forth as the undisputed dictator of Missouri's democracy." Yet in the same edition, the paper praised Truman with the comment: "Jackson County has found him a capable and honest public official, a man of unimpeachable character and integrity."

Throughout the nation, newspapers played up the story of the county judge who had won nomination to the U.S. Senate. Truman was not made happy by their conclusion that he was merely the tool of a boss. His childhood friend, Charlie Ross, was now chief of the editorial page of the St. Louis *Post-Dispatch,* which had backed Cochran, and an editorial in this paper gloomily noted: "Under our political system, an obscure man can be made the nominee of a major political party for the high office of United States Senator by virtue of the support given him by a city boss."

Nor were Truman's spirits given a lift when a *Post-Dispatch* reporter asked Pendergast: "Do you exact any promises in advance?" The boss's quick reply was: "If a candidate hasn't got sense enough to see who helped him win and hasn't sense enough to recognize that man's friends, there is no use asking for favors from that candidate in advance."

No one was surprised when Truman defeated Republican Senator Roscoe Patterson by 262,000 votes in the November general election. This was a Roosevelt year and the Republicans did not expect to win. Afterward, *The New York Times* wrote a sarcastic editorial titled "Just a Farmer Boy" about Truman, whom they referred to as "Judge Henry S. Truman" instead of Harry.

Shortly before he left Independence for Washington, townspeople held a banquet in his honor at a local church. Miss Anna Watson, postmistress of Marceline, made one of the speeches and she told Truman, "Someday you will be elected President and I will be there to see you inaugurated." Truman laughed uproariously at her prediction.

He also visited Tom Pendergast whose advice was blunt: "Work hard, keep your mouth shut and answer your mail." He then called on the Palmers, who were his high school principal and teacher. He talked to them about the history books he had been reading, his continuing interest in Latin and his hope to enroll at the Georgetown University Law School.

At noon on January 3, 1935, Truman walked down the Senate aisle attired in a rented morning coat and striped pants and was sworn in as a Senator. He had read a variety of biographies and magazine articles about his colleagues before coming to Washington and he was struck by the fact that most were college graduates and had better political backgrounds than he. It must have been the look of awe on his face that led Senator Hamilton Lewis, the Democratic whip from Illinois, to approach his desk in the back row of the Senate. "Mr. Truman," Senator Lewis began, "don't start out with an inferiority complex. For the first six months you'll wonder how you got here. After that you'll wonder how the rest of us got here."

But Truman suffered from more than a sense of intellectual inferiority. "I was under a cloud," he admitted. He realized that his colleagues and the Administration considered him to be the puppet of a corrupt political machine. Even when he had asked Victor Messall, an astute Capitol Hill employee, to serve as his aide, Messall had at first declined. "I told myself I'd lose my reputation if I worked for him," Messall said.

But Messall had agreed to help him find an apartment for his family and took him to a store to buy furniture on the installment plan. Then they stopped at a music store "where Truman sat down and played every piano in the place before he rented one for five dollars a month." Messall had time by now to observe him closely and he said, "My original impression of him was all wet. This was a man of real integrity and brains and no Pendergast or anyone else was going to push him around. Once you got to know him you knew he had something special. So I agreed to go to work for him."

On February 3, 1934, President Roosevelt had appointed Maurice Milligan, brother of Tuck Milligan who had been Truman's primary opponent, as U.S. attorney for the Western District of Missouri. Unknown to Truman, Maurice Milligan had been told to clean up Kansas City and break up the Pendergast empire.

It is little wonder, then, that Truman found that he was not warmly received by the Administration. When he paid a call on Henry Morgenthau, the Secretary of the Treasury, he failed to meet Morgenthau. "He was out—or maybe he just wouldn't let us in," said Truman. He also called the White House to make an appointment with President Roosevelt, whom he respected highly. However, for five months each request for a meeting was unsuccessful. There was concern at the White House that he wanted to handle matters with the President for Pendergast. "Actually," Messall said, "Senator Truman only wanted to meet Roosevelt to say hello and for no other reason. When we finally went to the White House for the appointment, several Cabinet members were sitting in the outer office and talking government business. However, none of them said hello to the Senator and he sat in silence while he waited. Finally, he went in to see the President, and though he had a fifteen-minute appointment he was out in only seven minutes."

Thus did Truman start his Senate career, as the man looked down upon by his colleagues and the Administration. Had anyone predicted then that he would one day rank as one of the most popular and highly regarded Senators as well as the heir apparent of the Roosevelt Administration, he would have evoked strange smiles.

12

---◆---

THROUGH THE
COMMITTEE ROPES

"Senator Truman may have come into the Senate under a cloud, but he had nothing to worry about," said Messall. "In the first place, he had a pleasing personality. He was always pleasant and made friends easily. He was always going out of his way to do favors for others and you couldn't help but like his smiling, friendly manner. In addition, he was a hard-working Senator and it was only a matter of time before he won acceptance from almost all the other Senators."

On the Democratic side of the aisle, Truman was fortunate in becoming an early protégé of Vice-President John N. Garner, who had served in Congress since 1903. Garner not only gave him the benefit of his long experience with fatherly advice on his work but also let him take over the Vice-President's chair on frequent occasions and preside over the Senate. Truman also had the help of Senator Carl Hayden, who had come to Congress when Arizona became a state in 1912. It was Hayden who tutored him on the complex Senate procedures. But Truman's closest friends were the "Young Turks," the twelve Democrats who were sworn in the same time he was.

As a Senator, Truman rose each morning at 5:30 A.M., read the newspapers and took a long brisk walk through Rock Creek Park. Once in his office, he went over the mail, talked to visitors and made calls to government agencies for Missourians who asked for his aid. "No lobbyist could ever demand anything from him or tell him how to vote," said Messall. "If anyone put pressure on him he immediately turned stubborn."

As for pressure on Truman from Tom Pendergast, Messall noted, "Pendergast never sent the Senator a single letter on legislation. His demands were much more insignificant. He would tear off a scrap of paper from a grocery bag and scribble a note in red pencil asking Truman for a favor. And his requests were never more important than for Truman to find a little clerk's job for people from Missouri."

This sort of request Truman did not consider as pressure, for he instinctively was in favor of helping all underdogs. For instance, one morning he and Messall were examining fifty folders of applications for appointments to West Point. The folders contained recommendation after recommendation from judges, state legislators and other prominent Missourians. Finally the two men opened a folder that held only a single-page application written in pencil on a sheet of cheap, rough paper. "We'll give this boy the appointment," Truman said.

At ten A.M. Truman hurried from his office to committee meetings and investigations. Then at noon he took his place

at his back row desk in the Senate chamber. He did not introduce his first bill for four months and it was only after six
months' service that he rose for the first time to speak. He
was a notoriously poor speaker and had to steel himself to
join in debate. As a rule he read prepared statements and
avoided give-and-take word exchanges. However, there was
one happy occasion when he entered the chamber while a
hectic debate was in progress.

Senator Arthur Vandenberg of Michigan, one of the con-
testants, interrupted the debate and called on Truman for
his opinion. "I happened to have the information that was
needed to settle the argument completely," said Truman.
When he finished, Vandenberg told the Senate, "When the
Senator from Missouri makes a statement like that we can
take it for the truth."

Senate debate often continued into the early evening.
Afterward Truman returned to Room 248, his three-room
suite in the Senate Office Building, to sign mail. He did not
get home for dinner until seven-thirty or eight, and sometimes after eating he went to the grocery or dried the dishes.
There was frequently an after-dinner period for piano playing, a time for running through a bit of his large repertoire
of Mozart and Chopin, his favorite composers. Daughter
Margaret, who was eleven when the family came to Washington, remembered that her father "brought home mountains of work and long after I was in bed he would be
reading and studying his problems."

Despite his rigorous work schedule, Truman managed an
enormous amount of personal reading on history, politics
and biographies. His special interest in the Civil War was
frequently revealed in the letters he wrote during this period.
For instance, he wrote to a Mr. Foster in New York: "I am

still studying battlefields. If you haven't done it you ought to compare Hillaire Belloc's outline of the Battle of Auster-litz (1805) with Chancellorsville (1863). You will be surprised at the similarity of the two maneuvers."

In the summer when Congress adjourned, he took the train back to Independence and joined his family at the big house on Delaware Street. He maintained an office in the Federal Building in Kansas City, but he took time off to drive to Grandview to see the "Old Rebel," as he affectionately called his mother who was now in her eighties. Martha Truman wrote him frequently during congressional sessions, expressing her views on bills before Congress. She also corresponded with several other Senators, pressing them to give greater support to her hero, President Franklin Roosevelt. She read the Congressional Record daily and congratulated her son when she thought he voted right and criticized him when he did not.

To Truman, the most interesting and vital part of his Senate day was the hours he spent in committee. Here opposing witnesses came to testify and face questioning from Senators on matters ranging from the way the government was operating to the need for new laws. "I found out very soon after I settled down to a study of my duties," he said, "that the business of a good legislator is not to get things done quickly but to prevent, if possible, the enactment into the law of the land many crazy and crackpot measures."

One of the committees he served on was the Appropriations Committee, which determined how much money the government could spend and for what purposes. Because of his own military experience and interest, Truman specialized in defense and military spending on this committee. Despite the threat to world peace by Adolf Hitler's Germany, the United States was pacifist-minded at the time. Truman found himself in a small minority in urging a larger American Army to be ready for any eventuality.

He also served on the Printing Committee, which supervised the Government Printing Office, the Public Buildings and Grounds Committee and the Interstate Commerce Committee. It was his work on this last committee that was to gain him his first prominence.

The man who did most to give him this prominence was Senator Burton K. Wheeler, chairman of the Interstate Commerce Committee. Wheeler, the tenth son of a poor New England shoemaker, had gone west to Montana after graduating from law school. His work as a U.S. district attorney provided him with a springboard to the Senate in 1923, where he soon gained a national reputation as a fearless investigator of improper government relations with private business.

When Truman first joined Wheeler's committee, the lanky Montana Senator was then investigating large private investment firms, known as "holding companies," that controlled the electrical power industry. When Wheeler proposed a bill forcing the holding companies to give up their control over the electric companies, Truman found himself under immediate pressure from the holding companies. They sent lobbyists who baldly threatened his political future and they swamped his office with 30,000 letters of protest. But Truman ordered the letters burned and denounced the lobbyists.

As a result of Truman's stand, Wheeler put him on a three-man subcommittee to write a law to regulate the nonmilitary aviation industry. From these hearings came the Civil Aeronautics Act of 1938, the basic law under which this industry still operates today.

The most important activity Truman engaged in during his first term in the Senate came about by accident. In December 1936, Wheeler began an investigation of the railroad industry, which was plagued by holding companies who were using the industry's income to enrich themselves. In the process, many lines had gone bankrupt and others limped along with old, dirty equipment and with little regard to passenger and freight conveniences.

Truman had hoped to win a seat on the railroad investigations subcommittee, but Wheeler did not make him a member. Noting Truman's disappointment, however, Wheeler agreed to permit him to sit in the hearings as an observer.

Reporters who covered this investigation said that "for two years this inquiry plodded along through some of the dullest hearings ever recorded on Capitol Hill." Hundreds of witnesses appeared from the various railroads and month after month discussed highly complicated and dry financial data. Some of the subcommittee members failed to attend the hearings after a while, but Truman never missed a session. In fact, he began his own private study of the railroad industry to gain a better understanding of what was being discussed. Often he spent evenings at the Library of Congress, scanning old newspaper files and reading every available book on railroad history and management. On one occasion, he had the Library send him fifty books concerning the railroads and he plowed through them methodically.

In time, one of the subcommittee members resigned and Wheeler named Truman to replace him. Then all the other members took to skipping the hearings and Truman found himself running the investigation singlehandedly. Wheeler now named him vice-chairman.

Lobbyists appeared in his office with threats and bags of

mail poured in demanding that he call off the investigation. But Truman was not easily frightened. "Don't ease up on anything," he told his staff. Max Lowenthal, his staff director, later told a reporter, "There were not two other Senators who would have withstood such political pressure as Senator Truman did."

Truman now gained an ally in the person of Louis D. Brandeis, Associate Justice of the Supreme Court. Brandeis was noted as the scholar on the Court as well as the opponent of bigness in government and in industry. He opposed monopolies and preached constantly about the blessings of small business and free competition.

Brandeis, who was then in his eighties, held weekly teas in his Washington apartment. Lowenthal brought Truman there one time and the elderly gentleman took an immediate liking to the Senator, insisting that he henceforth become a regular caller. It was an experience for Truman to listen to top lawyers discuss the Constitution and to sit among economists who presented complex theories on what was needed to end the depression. "I'm not used to meeting people like that," Truman said humbly after his first visit.

But after a few more visits he felt at home and joined in the discussions. "The old man would back me into a corner," he said, "and pay no attention to anyone else while he talked transportation to me." Brandeis also discussed the "curse of bigness" with Truman, and his influence on the Senator was great.

This can readily be seen in the first full speeches Truman delivered on the Senate floor in June and December of 1937. "Some of the country's greatest railroads have been deliberately looted by their financial agents," he said. "Jesse James held up the Missouri Pacific in 1876 and took the paltry sum of $17,000 from the express car. About thirty years later some gentlemen known as the 'Tin Plate Millionaires' ruined the Rock Island Railroad and got away with $70,000,000. They did it by means of holding companies." In his December speech he said, "I believe the country would be better off if we did not have 60 percent of the assets of all insurance companies concentrated in only four companies. I also say that a thousand towns of 7,000 people each are a thousand times more important to this Republic than one city of seven million people." Brandeis was one of the first to congratulate him.

In January 1939, Truman finally completed the hearings. First he told the Senate why a new law was needed to regulate the finances of the railroads. Then he and Lowenthal sat down and wrote it. Passage did not come quickly because the holding companies exerted tremendous pressure on Congress to defeat the bill. In May 1940, Truman said, "I feel as if my four years and a half of hard work has been practically wasted, but we will be ready for a new start when Congress next meets."

It was not until that fall that the Transportation Act of 1940 became law. When President Roosevelt signed the bill, his approval marked Truman's final acceptance by his Senate colleagues as an important member. Senator George Norris of Nebraska, one of the Senate's all-time greats, who had avoided any association with Truman, was to say: "I watched him in the public service more than I otherwise would, and I must say that in all the time I knew him, I never knew of an instance, I knew of no time that the bosses or the machine controlled his official work. I think he has done some very good work."

13

---◆◆◆---

FIGHT FOR REELECTION

Despite Truman's success as a Senator, he was in serious political trouble when 1940 arrived. At the very time he had marched down the Senate aisle to be sworn in back in 1935, Tom Pendergast had begun a chain of action that was to ruin the Missouri boss and endanger Truman's political future. All of it had now come home to make 1940 Truman's most crucial political year.

The trouble began with Pendergast's passion for betting on horse races. Since early manhood he had spent many an afternoon at the track, but with the passing years his bets increased and his losses grew enormous. Government records revealed, for instance, that in 1935 he bet two million dollars and lost $600,000.

If ever a man gave up his kingdom for a horse it was Tom Pendergast. Gambling became a disease that he could not control and as his losses mounted, he grew desperate in seeking ways to pay off his racing debts. One year City Manager McElroy recorded large false payments for rental equipment and passed the money to Pendergast. Another year he entered into the city's records a payment of $365,000 to check into leaks in the city's water mains. No such check was ever made, but the money went to Pendergast.

At the beginning of 1935, Pendergast was so desperate that he did not go to Washington to watch Truman being sworn in as Senator. Instead, he traveled to Chicago for a conversation about a bribe that would eventually lead to his downfall. Back in 1929, 137 insurance companies had raised fire insurance rates in Missouri by $16\frac{2}{3}$ percent. However, a federal court had impounded the money realized by this increase and ordered it held until the court decided where the money should go. By 1935, the impounded money totaled almost ten million dollars. The insurance companies were anxious to get a favorable court decision, and reasoning that Pendergast's political influence could bring this about, they asked him to come to a meeting at the Palmer House in Chicago.

There was no turning back for Pendergast once he walked into the hotel room on January 22, 1935. He needed what money he could lay his hands on. At first he sneered at a bribe of $200,000 for a favorable settlement. When he rose to leave, the bribe was raised to $500,000. The final offer which he agreed to was $750,000. But before he left the hotel room, he asked to use the phone, and called a bookie with whom he placed a bet on a horse race.

After Pendergast received his first $100,000, his agent, Emmett O'Malley, the Missouri state superintendent of insurance, made a settlement which the court accepted in February 1936. The court awarded 80 percent of the impounded money to the insurance companies and shortly afterward Pendergast received his next bribe installment of $250,000. He was certain that the bribe would never be uncovered, because payments were made in cash.

At this time, Maurice Milligan, who had been named by President Roosevelt to destroy the Pendergast machine, was busy looking for leads. By June 1936, when the Democratic National Convention met in Philadelphia, he had yet to uncover any evidence.

Senator Truman was there as a delegate and Tom Pendergast was the boss of the Missouri delegation. Pendergast did not get an opportunity to voice his opposition to a second term for President Roosevelt because on the opening day of the convention he suffered sharp pains in his upper abdomen. Truman took him to New York that evening and doctors diagnosed his trouble as a heart attack. Later, in the hospital, they discovered he had intestinal cancer. The operation proved successful, but he was required to remain in New York for a long recuperation. Had he died on the operating table, there is little question that Milligan would have ended his investigation.

He did not die, however, and Milligan pursued his activities. His first break came with the primary election in August. With Pendergast away, his lieutenants worked doubly hard to keep the Goat machine intact. They made a sweeping victory at the Democratic primary polls by falsifying the list of eligible voters with 60,000 ghost voters. For instance, they entered votes for hundreds of dead persons, listed 141 persons as living in a single house and 112 as residents of a vacant lot.

One of the persons whose election they insured was Lloyd Stark who was running for governor. Pendergast had originally opposed Stark's candidacy, but at Truman's insistence belatedly gave him his blessing. "The registration was crooked in 1936," said Truman, "and that was what made Stark governor. I don't believe Tom Pendergast knew anything about it. It was due to overzealousness of his workers, the desire to make a big showing."

Shortly after Stark moved into the governor's mansion, he decided to work with Milligan to overthrow the Pendergast machine. In 1937, he appointed a new elections board which removed the 60,000 ghost votes from Jackson County and established a plan to prevent a recurrence. At the same time Milligan won indictments against Pendergast aides and 259 Goats were convicted of illegal activities in the 1936 primary.

Despite Roosevelt's advertised intention of destroying Pendergast, the President did not shrink from asking for his aid. And despite the boss's hatred of Roosevelt, he sometimes complied because he thought this might lessen the attack upon him by the Administration. In July 1937, for instance, James Farley, the Postmaster General, asked Pendergast to phone Truman and "line up Harry on the right side." The Senate was to vote for a new majority leader and Roosevelt's candidate was Senator Alben Barkley, who was opposed by Senator Pat Harrison.

"Look here, Harry," Pendergast said over the phone. "Jim Farley just called and asked me if I couldn't talk to you about voting for Barkley. Can't you do that?"

"No, Tom, I can't," Truman replied. "I've given my word to Pat Harrison."

That was enough for Pendergast. "Well, Harry," he said, "I told Jim you were the contrariest guy in the world. So I guess that's that."

Barkley won by a vote of 38 to 37, and he said afterward,

"I have often wondered how I would have felt about Harry Truman if I had lost the majority leadership by one vote!"

Milligan's four-year term as U.S. attorney ended early in 1938 and Governor Stark demanded that he be reappointed to a second term. Truman made a long speech to the Senate attacking Milligan, but he ended by saying, "Because the President asked for him, I have not exercised the usual senatorial prerogative to block his confirmation." So Milligan was free to continue his investigation of Pendergast.

It was in the summer of 1938 that Pendergast's secret insurance bribe came to light. A clerk in the Internal Revenue Bureau told a Kansas City reporter about some insurance company checks that had been cashed in Chicago and the money turned over to an unidentified Missouri politician. The reporter told Governor Stark about it and Stark relayed the story to Milligan. Then Stark went to Washington where he discussed this with President Roosevelt and soon the government's best legal brains were put to work with Milligan to break the case.

In early 1939, Pendergast was aware that government agents were particularly busy in Kansas City. In March when Truman was in the city, it was obvious to him that Pendergast was in serious trouble, though the boss would not discuss it with him. He was on his way back to Washington when a reporter told him that Pendergast had been indicted. Here was Truman's opportunity to throw off the machine and denounce Pendergast, but his sense of loyalty and feeling of debt were too strong. "I am very sorry to hear it," he told the reporter. "I know nothing about the details, nor why the indictment was voted. Tom Pendergast has always been my friend and I don't desert a sinking ship."

In the court action that followed, Judge Merrill Otis sentenced Pendergast to fifteen months in federal prison, fined him $10,000, ordered him to pay $434,000 for income-tax evasion and said that he must refrain from any political activity for five years. He was soon on his way to Leavenworth, his political dynasty at an end.

After the prison gates closed behind Pendergast, newspapers insisted that Stark run for Truman's Senate seat in 1940. President Roosevelt also announced that Stark would make an admirable addition to the Washington scene. Senator James F. Byrnes, who went to the White House and urged the President to stay out of the Missouri contest, said afterward, "The President told me that while he did not know much about Mr. Truman, Governor Stark was an intimate friend, was very progressive and would make a great Senator." As for Truman, said Victor Messall, his aide, "Roosevelt tried to get Truman to accept an appointment to the Interstate Commerce Committee. He told him he didn't have a chance to be reelected."

Truman's angry reply was "that if I received only one vote I intended to make the fight for vindication and reelection to the Senate."

Governor Stark announced his candidacy for Truman's seat in September 1939, shortly after Nazi Germany invaded Poland. Not long afterward came a surprise. Maurice Milligan, who had teamed up with Stark to get Pendergast, also announced his candidacy. He said that some of Truman's own friends asked him to run and he added, "How could a Pendergast man get anywhere without a Pendergast?"

Truman little realized how poor were his chances until he asked thirty friends to meet with him in St. Louis in January 1940 to discuss plans for a second six-year term as Senator. Only a handful of the thirty came. "Much worse," said Messall, "all those present told him he didn't have a chance of winning."

At this point, Truman decided not to run and returned to Washington. Messall had stayed behind in Missouri and with the filing day deadline drawing near, he telephoned Truman. "Look, Senator, if you don't file you can't be elected. If you don't run you're through in politics."

"It takes from one hundred to one hundred and fifty dollars to file," Truman said. "I've got to think about it."

"There's no time," Messall cut in.

Truman was silent a long time. Finally he said, "All right, Vic, go ahead and file for me."

In a heavy February snowstorm, Messall drove to Jefferson City and deposited the necessary filing amount with the Secretary of State just before the doors closed at noon that Saturday. "I didn't think Harry was going to file," the official gasped.

Truman fully realized the great odds against his winning the Democratic primary against Stark and Milligan. In the first place, the stigma of having been associated with Tom Pendergast was a great disadvantage, even though it was accepted generally in Missouri that he had not taken part in the machine's dirty work. Second, he had no money to finance a proper campaign. Then he lacked organized support, and fourth, almost every newspaper in the state opposed him strenuously.

The best headquarters Messall could afford was an old dilapidated building at Sedalia, Missouri. He realized that people were fond of titles and he was able to acquire a campaign committee of sorts by giving each person the title of vice-chairman. For his campaign treasurer and money raiser, Truman selected his war buddy, Harry Vaughan. "There were a half-dozen bankers for whom Truman had done great financial favors," said Vaughan. "But they couldn't be located. It was a joke when the campaign committee named me treasurer. They were looking for someone with a title and I was a lieutenant colonel in the Reserve Corps. I was then a salesman and I had a bank balance of a dollar and a quarter."

Without newspaper support, Truman knew that his campaign depended on his ability to get around the state and make speeches. His eighty-eight-year-old mother sat on the platform when he made his opening speech at Sedalia on June 15. The "Old Rebel" had an uncanny ability to judge who on the platform was for her son and who merely pretended, and she frankly told him so. Paris had surrendered to Hitler's Nazis the day before and the atmosphere in Sedalia was grim. But the show had to go and after several speakers praised Truman, he rose and began his speech. Dr. W. L. Brandon, one of his eleven campaign committee vice-chairmen, remarked upon his conclusion that he was "such a bad speaker that it was pitiful." However, Truman's sincerity pleased the crowd, as did his talk about the brotherhood of man—"Not merely the brotherhood of white men but the brotherhood of all men before law."

As he set off on an automobile tour of 75 counties, the St. Louis *Post-Dispatch* quickly derided his effort as useless. An editorial cartoon showed two huge trucks, one labeled Milligan and the other Stark, in a head-on collision with Truman caught in a kiddycar between them.

However, Truman realized that his situation was not that hopeless. In the first place, Stark foolishly delayed his campaign because he expected President Roosevelt to name him as his running mate for a third term at the Democratic National Convention that summer. By the time the convention selected Henry Wallace instead for Vice-President, he had already lost precious weeks. As for Milligan, he proved to be a worse speaker than Truman and his gangbuster personality failed to come across to his listeners.

Nevertheless, as July moved along Truman faced serious crises. When his campaign funds were exhausted, he borrowed $3,000 on his life insurance policy. But this was soon gone. In addition, the papers were deliberately omitting any mention of his speeches.

Less than two weeks before the primary, Harry Vaughan had only $200 in cash and several outstanding debts to pay. At this point of desperation, he decided on a gamble, and spent the entire $200 on 1½¢ stamps. These he attached to 13,300 open-flapped envelopes he already possessed and sent them to voters with the message: "If you want to see Harry Truman returned to the Senate, send $1 immediately." Back came $1,800 and he invested all of this in further letters. This time he gained enough money to pay off his bills and keep Truman's campaign alive.

The question of newspaper publicity remained hopeless until the Railroad Brotherhoods unions came out for Truman. Hurriedly, they issued a special Truman edition of *Labor,* the Brotherhoods' paper, and flooded the state with more than a half-million copies.

As the campaign moved into its final week, Truman's stock was up. Yet his followers agreed that he could not win without a good showing in St. Louis. The Democratic machine there was controlled by Mayor Bernard Dickmann and Robert Hannegan, who were backing Stark. Truman's aides now began putting pressure on Hannegan to throw his support to Truman. Only two days before the primary, Hannegan agreed by ordering his precinct workers to ring doorbells and promote Truman without letup.

Early returns on August 6 showed Stark far in the lead. By ten P.M. Truman was 11,000 votes behind and his committee was ready to admit defeat. "I went to bed defeated," Truman later admitted.

But in the middle of the night, as more votes were counted, Stark's lead began to dwindle. Then came the St. Louis total. Truman, who was supposed to be without a following in that city, captured the election there by 8,411 votes. This was sufficient to give him a final lead of about 8,000 votes over Stark throughout the state. Bob Hannegan had made his victory possible.

There was still the general election in November against Manvelle Davis, the Republican candidate. But this was anticlimactic, considering what Truman had gone through in the primary. He defeated Davis by a vote of 930,775 to 886,376.

In his flush of triumph, Truman bore no grudges. Milligan had resigned as U.S. attorney to run against him in the primary. Truman now wrote to President Roosevelt asking that he be reappointed. "He has made a good district attorney, and I do not feel that he ought to be penalized by losing his job."

To Truman, 1940 was the most trying year of his life. But it was also the year of his vindication. When he returned to the Senate following his grueling experience, his colleagues treated him to a wild, standing ovation. A reporter wrote: "They behaved like boys greeting a popular schoolmate who had just got over the measles."

He now belonged in the Senate on his own merit, independent and secure, no longer the creature of Tom Pendergast.

14

---❖---

THE TRUMAN COMMITTEE

B<small>Y THE CLOSE</small> of 1940, Hitler's military success in Europe had shaken the United States from its philosophy of isolation. President Roosevelt began his third term with strenuous efforts to change the depression-stunted American economy into an "arsenal of democracy." Defense contracts totaling twenty-five billion dollars were offered to industry; aid started to flow to beleagured England standing alone against the Nazis; and a large American military force passed from the blueprint stage to active mobilization.

At the beginning of 1941, Truman heard about the appalling waste in the construction of Fort Leonard Wood at Rolla, Missouri. He was soon behind the driver's wheel of his coupe and on his way for a firsthand investigation. He found confusion everywhere—workers sleeping on the job, contractors interested solely in profits and valuable equipment dumped outdoors unprotected from the elements.

Before returning to Washington, he completed a 30,000-

mile tour of defense plants and other Army camps under
construction. "The trip was an eye-opener," he said. As the
man who had kept such close watch over Jackson County's
road building and courthouse construction, he was shocked
by the enormous national waste he saw.

His anger was so great that on February 10, 1941, he rose
in the Senate chamber and denounced the budding defense
program, pointing out its gross shortcomings. Nowhere had
he found any indications that the government was protect-
ing its interests. "It won't do any good digging up dead
horses after the war is over," he warned. "The thing to do
is dig up this stuff now and correct it." What was needed
was a senatorial committee to investigate the operations of
the vast defense program, and he introduced Senate Resolution 71 to provide this.

On March 1, the Senate agreed to the establishment of a
special defense investigations committee and Truman was
named chairman. However, the Senate's leaders proposed
several severe limitations. First, it was expected that Truman
would limit his investigation to Fort Leonard Wood, and for
this reason his committee was granted a paltry $15,000. In
addition, Truman was not given a free hand in the selection
of his six committee associates.

Despite these and other limitations, Truman set out on
his task. From the outset, he had no intention of restricting
his investigation to the Missouri camp. As he viewed his
committee's role, its job was to look into the entire national
defense program. This meant investigating the buying of
materials and supplies and the construction and operation
of defense plants and military camps.

He realized that his limitation of funds might prove highly
restrictive and he sought ways to stretch his dollars to collect

a superior staff. One of his first acts was to ask Attorney General Robert Jackson to send him his best lawyer, a young, energetic, brilliant and hard-hitting man. Jackson sent Hugh Fulton, a large, heavy man in his midthirties, who wore a derby and possessed a squeaky voice. Fulton had an excellent record as a government prosecutor and Truman agreed to give him a salary of $9,000. This left him with only $6,000, hardly enough for a few stenographers. But Truman got around this problem by "borrowing" personnel at no cost from government agencies until he had his staff of fifteen lawyers and investigators.

When his committee first met, Truman had to determine what its approach and purpose would be in conducting its investigations. Some Senators proposed that he run a super type of House Un-American Activities Committee, examining the personal integrity of government defense officials as well as the operations of contractors. Others suggested that the committee examine and criticize the programs of the military chiefs of staff. Said Senator Harley Kilgore of the committee, "Senator Truman and I had several discussions on the activities of the Civil War's Joint Committee on the Conduct of the War. This congressional committee not only interfered with military operations and strategy, which prolonged the Civil War unnecessarily and at great cost in lives, but it also tried to do Lincoln in. Lee later said that the Joint Committee was worth several divisions to him."

"Thank goodness, I knew my history," said Truman, "and I wouldn't make a Committee on the Conduct of the War out of my committee." Instead, he pointedly told his colleagues that the committee would never enter into problems relating to military strategy or on the size or disposal of military forces or weapons. Its sole purpose would be to investigate the manner in which the defense program was proceeding and to uncover graft, waste and inefficiency. It would deal only in facts and work to have shortcomings corrected.

Truman also established other rules. "He functioned as a chief of staff," said Kilgore, "and he was a good one. He welded the committee members together as a team." He insisted that anything the committee accomplished would be made public as the work of the entire committee and not the handiwork of individual members. No member was to seek headlines or individual glory. The work of the committee would be reported solely on the Senate floor or in formal documents, not as individual interviews with reporters. All committee reports were to have the unanimous approval of the members before being released. This last rule seemed ridiculous in view of the fact that so many shades of opinion were represented on the committee. Yet it worked in practice! Said Republican Senator Owen Brewster of the committee, when this proved to be the case, "Reasonable men don't differ when they have the facts."

With these standards in mind, the Truman Committee began its work. First it heard Cabinet members involved in the defense program who provided the general picture. Then came government officials and military officers directly involved in various programs. After this, the committee took to the road to see for itself what was going on in the camp construction program.

Members examined nine camps closely and in August 1941 came the committee's first report. This was a 98-page document noting the "needless waste" of more than $100 million in the billion-dollar camp construction program. Truman charged that the Army had used "fantastically poor judgment" and had handed out money to contractors and engi-

neers "much the same way that Santa Claus passes out gifts."
The report was so filled with detailed examples that the
Army later admitted that the changes it brought about as a
result of the report saved the government $200 million.

With the publication of this report out of the way, Truman
and his committee held hearings and roamed the country,
going through shipyards, mines, aircraft factories, defense
housing developments, machine tool plants and other defense
works. By December, the committee had already held 70
hearings, heard hundreds of witnesses and collected more
than 3,000 pages of testimony. In Washington, the committee
met in the "doghouse," a room in Truman's office, where
they discussed their activities and went over proposed reports.
Defense officials also came to the "doghouse," where Truman
gave them the opportunity to change their irregular activities or face the publication of reports. Sometimes individuals
came with ideas for improving the defense program. Some
were silly, but the committee heard them all. One man proposed filling airplanes with dirt and dumping them on enemy
capitals, which, he insisted, would bury those cities.

On Sunday afternoon, December 7, 1941, Truman was
asleep in a small hotel in Columbia, Missouri, after a hectic
week. His wife telephoned him from Washington with news
about the Japanese attack on Pearl Harbor. When he finally
returned to Washington, it was Monday noon and President
Roosevelt was preparing to tell Congress "hostilities exist."
Three days later when Germany and Italy declared war on
the United States, the fighting became global.

Truman's first reaction was to join the regular Army and
resign from the Senate, and he hurried to see General
George C. Marshall. But Marshall would not hear of this.
"Senator, you've got a big job to do with your investigating

committee," he turned Truman aside. "Besides, this is a young man's war. We don't need old stiffs like you."

"I am younger than you," Truman told the sixty-one-year old general.

"Yes, but I'm a general and you'd be only a colonel. You stay where you are."

Disappointed though he was, Truman returned to his senatorial duties and plunged into the writing of his committee's most important report so far. He had found that the government agencies directing the war program were botching their job. The primary reasons were their disorganization and divided leadership. Truman proposed to end this chaotic situation by bringing the work together under a single director with authority to act on his decisions.

Before making his report public, he sent it first to Roosevelt, who acted immediately on Truman's recommendations by establishing the War Production Board with Donald Nelson as chairman. Only afterward did Truman read his 146-page report to the Senate. The President, appreciative of his gesture, now made an effort to begin a closer relationship with the Senator.

In 1942, the Senate gave the Truman Committee $100,000 to expand its work, and Truman roamed the country anew on trains. His frequent traveling companion was Senator Kilgore, and the two would flip a coin to see who would sleep in the lower berth. That year, even more staggering evidence of waste and corruption was uncovered. Besides exposing these conditions, the committee was also responsible for saving many lives. For instance, the committee found that one large aircraft firm was producing defective war planes that resulted in the deaths of several student pilots. The committee condemned four hundred engines and the company was forced to produce safer models.

In 1943, the Truman Committee looked into the seaworthiness of Liberty cargo vessels, lend-lease operations with British and Russian allies, postwar reconversion of American industry and the renegotiation of war contracts. That year also one of Truman's investigators chanced upon the secret work on the atomic bomb. Truman was all set to investigate the $2 billion expenditure when a White House official called on him and explained why he should not get into this activity.

By 1944, the Truman Committee had become part of the American vocabulary. To the citizens of the nation the committee meant honest, forthright investigating and exposure of crooks. To the Senate, Truman was known as the "fact" man, who carried more correct information in his head about the operation of the war economy than any other man. On one occasion a memo went out from his office which referred to the "47 states." A reporter said, "If Harry Truman says there are 47 states, you'd better look in the morning paper to see which one has seceded."

Reporters gave wide publicity to the committee whose work had cost only $400,000 but whose investigations had saved the nation $15 billion. The St. Louis *Post-Dispatch*, which had been his severest critic in the past, called him "one of the most useful and at the same time one of the most forthright and fearless of the ninety-six Senators." The *Reader's Digest* praised the Truman Committee as "the public's most accessible court of appeals, the sharpest prod and one of the most powerful action-getting agencies in the government." In the spring of 1944, a poll of Washington reporters named Truman as the man next to President Roosevelt who had contributed most to the war effort.

The Truman Committee had served as the vehicle to propel Truman to the forefront of his country's political figures. He was suddenly in demand as a speaker, and though he made some speeches he refused any payment. Reporters eagerly sought out his views and some said he had somehow changed from the man who had nervously come to the Senate back in 1935. "I haven't changed," Truman insisted. "I am the same person I was five or ten years ago." He had not changed; he had grown through breadth of experience.

15

———◈———

RISE TO VICE-PRESIDENT

THE YEAR 1944 was to prove a turning point in Truman's career. As it started, President Roosevelt was busily engaged in planning the forthcoming Normandy invasion for June; Truman was hurrying about the country on his investigations; and Democratic party leaders were laying the groundwork for the July Democratic National Convention in Chicago.

Two problems plagued the party's bosses as they held preliminary talks. First, they did not believe they could win unless Roosevelt ran for an unprecedented fourth term. Yet Roosevelt gave no indication that he would. Second, they were in agreement that Vice-President Henry Wallace was a voting detriment in the South and should be dropped from the ticket. However, Roosevelt was fond of Wallace.

At first, the Democratic leaders did not consider Truman as a possible replacement for Wallace, even though he was in the public eye. With his obvious ability as an administrator, they offered him instead the post of chairman of the Democratic National Committee. This would have placed him in close association with Roosevelt in running the party's organization.

Truman was flattered by the offer, but he rejected it with a counterproposal that it go instead to Robert Hannegan, who had made possible his 1940 victory over Governor Stark. Hannegan, who was then forty-one, had been active in St. Louis politics ever since he took his law degree in 1925 at the age of twenty-two. Following his efforts in the 1940 Missouri race, Truman had helped him become Collector of Internal Revenue at St. Louis. Then in October 1943, he gave him an assist into the important job of Commissioner of Internal Revenue in Washington. His suggestion now that he be further elevated to head the Democratic National Committee was acceptable to the Democratic leaders, including the President, and he took over the National Committee on January 22, 1944. The selection of Hannegan was to be a vital factor in what was to follow.

Hardly had Hannegan assumed his new post when a great emergency overtook the party's leaders. "The question of the President's health!" Edward Flynn, Democratic boss of the Bronx, moaned. "Signs of failing health in the President were unmistakable." The President's skin had turned papery and he lacked pep. The bosses agreed he could not possibly last another four years, but he was still needed to win the next national election. They concluded that whoever was on the ticket with Roosevelt was bound to move into the White House before 1948. "You are not nominating a Vice-President of the United States, but a President!" said Edwin Pauley, the National Committee Treasurer.

Late in January the National Committee met with Roosevelt in the White House. They did not bring up the subject of a fourth term for fear he would reject it outright. Instead, they carefully restricted the conversation to Vice-Presidential possibilities. Every mention of Wallace's name was met with frowns, and each person Roosevelt mentioned received the treatment of headshaking and negative argument. Finally Hannegan brought up Truman's name and the bosses agreed he would be an admirable candidate. But Roosevelt made no comment.

In the months that followed, the party bosses worked hard to convince the President he must run again and that he must drop Wallace. The first task was not too difficult. Even though Roosevelt knew his health was slipping and once told Senator Kilgore, "The details of this job are killing me," he wanted to establish the United Nations and be on the scene to safeguard enduring world peace.

As to the second task, the bosses enlisted the aid of the White House appointments secretary. He agreed to make it difficult for Wallace supporters to see the President. In addition, he asked the anti-Wallace visitors to mention their disapproval of Wallace to the President. By spring, this campaign became effective because instead of defending Wallace, Roosevelt grew silent about his Vice-President. When Mrs. Roosevelt asked him to keep Wallace on the ticket, he replied, "If Wallace could not convince the party leaders that he was the right person, I cannot dictate to them twice." Then in May, Roosevelt took Wallace out of the crucial political maneuvering by requesting him to fly to war-torn China and Siberia on a diplomatic mission.

In the meantime, Hannegan was quietly at work building support for Truman. But Truman told reporters, "If Bob Hannegan is running me for Vice-President, he is doing it without my knowledge and without my consent. I'm happy in the Senate. I have my friends and I don't have any political ambitions." Hannegan went to him and patiently insisted that he make no more public statements taking himself from the race. Truman agreed, though he expressed his certainty that the President would never consider him.

After the long-awaited Normandy invasion of Europe took place on June 6, Hannegan grew aware that the tired President had shifted his support from Wallace to James F. Byrnes, the former Representative, Senator and Supreme Court Justice and now "Assistant President" as director of the Office of War Mobilization. Hannegan realized that since Byrnes saw the President daily, it would be a simple matter for Byrnes to ask Roosevelt for a public statement in his behalf. To prevent Byrnes from taking this move, Hannegan flatteringly told him he was behind him and would soon get the President to come out for Byrnes. The result was that Byrnes delayed speaking directly with Roosevelt.

The party bosses realized their first goal on July 10 when Roosevelt announced his candidacy for a fourth term. Then on the next evening they went to the White House for dinner to settle the Vice-Presidential issue. During the meal, Roosevelt would not discuss the matter of his running mate. It was only afterward when they joined him in his second-floor study that conversation turned to this question.

One by one, they canvassed potential Vice-Presidents. They would not discuss Wallace, and though they agreed that House Speaker Sam Rayburn was a good man, Rayburn was in serious political trouble because of a split among Texas Democrats. Roosevelt pushed aside Senator Alben Barkley on the grounds that he was five years older than he. When the President brought up John Winant, the ambassador to Great Britain, the group held to a cold silence. Then came Byrnes, whose name was treated to harsh objections.

The evening was racing past when Roosevelt suggested Supreme Court Justice William O. Douglas as a suitable running mate. "Douglas," said the President, "has the same kind of following Wallace has; he also has practical experience from the backwoods of the Northwest as a logger. He looks and acts on occasion like a Boy Scout—and besides, he plays an interesting game of poker." After an initial uneasiness, the group argued that Douglas had no visible supporters because he had never been in politics and would therefore be a liability on the ticket.

Hannegan now proposed Senator Truman and Flynn quickly pointed out his excellent record in Congress. Besides, Flynn recounted, Truman was highly respected by organized labor and he came from a border state and not from the South, a factor that would not antagonize Northern liberals. "Truman is the man who would hurt you least," Flynn closed his argument.

Roosevelt refused to accept the group's insistence on Truman without a struggle. He pointed out Truman's association with Tom Pendergast, though he agreed that Truman had never been found to have engaged in the Goat machine's wrongdoings. He then went on to say that while Truman had done a superior job with his investigating committee, he did not know him intimately. "And what about his age?" Roosevelt asked. "Truman must be about sixty while Douglas is under fifty."

A crisis was at hand when Roosevelt looked about his study for a book that would prove Truman's age. When he did not find what he sought, he asked John Boettiger, his son-in-law, to locate a Congressional Directory and look up Truman's age.

A pall settled over the room when Boettiger left to find the volume. The party bosses realized that Truman was sixty and if Roosevelt learned this he would eliminate the Senator from consideration. But Ed Pauley saved the day when Boettiger returned with the book. Pauley casually took the Congressional Directory from Boettiger's hand, laid it on his lap and started an animated conversation with Roosevelt to distract him. The ruse worked, for the President forgot about Truman's age and at the close of the meeting said to Hannegan, "Bob, I think you and everyone here want Truman."

A few days later Hannegan went to see the President, hoping he would put in writing that he preferred Truman. However, Roosevelt would not do this. Instead he gave him a letter that read: "You have written me about Bill Douglas and Harry Truman. I should, of course, be very glad to run with either of them."

Hannegan was displeased with the letter. Roosevelt had not only failed to single out Truman but he had placed Douglas's name before that of the Senator.

When the Democratic National Convention began on July 19, Truman arrived in Chicago pledged to support James Byrnes for Vice-President. Byrnes had never asked for a written statement from Roosevelt because Hannegan continued to tell him it was unnecessary, that the President and the party bosses were for him. Henry Wallace was also back from the Orient, fully aware that the bosses had been working on the President to disavow him. The most he had been able to get from Roosevelt was a letter to the convention that stated that if the President were a delegate he would vote for Wallace.

Chicago was stifling hot when Hannegan paid a call on Truman in his hotel suite. Hannegan insisted that Roosevelt wanted Truman for Vice-President. But Truman just as quickly replied that Byrnes had asked him to nominate him and had added, "FDR wants me to have that position on the ticket."

While Truman began his tour of the different delegations to promote Byrnes, Hannegan decided on a desperate maneuver. Roosevelt was then preparing to board his special train for the West Coast, where he would transfer to a ship for a Pearl Harbor conference with Admiral Chester Nimitz and General Douglas MacArthur. Roosevelt had intended to bypass the convention, but Hannegan called him and requested him to pause a short time in the Chicago railroad yard.

At three o'clock on a Saturday afternoon, Hannegan scampered aboard the Presidential train. He demanded to know whether Roosevelt was really supporting Byrnes, as Byrnes insisted he was. Roosevelt smiled this away, though he refused to give Hannegan a statement that he wanted Truman. Nevertheless, when Hannegan left the President's private car, he gave Grace Tully, Roosevelt's secretary, the "Bill Douglas and Harry Truman" letter Roosevelt had written earlier in the week. "Grace," he told her, "the President wants you to retype this letter and switch these names so it will read 'Harry Truman or Bill Douglas.'" Armed with this new letter, he left the train.

Truman met with little response in his effort to promote Byrnes. At breakfast, Sidney Hillman, the labor leader, told him that his organization, the C.I.O., was for Wallace. "There is only one other man we could consider supporting," he went on, "and I'm looking at him now."

The reaction was the same everywhere he went. Byrnes had no real support; Wallace was ahead but Truman was not far behind. Truman was embarrassed by his reception and dutifully reported his experiences to Byrnes. "It means nothing," Byrnes said. "At the proper time Roosevelt will say publicly he is for me."

The convention hall area became a scene of chaos as delegates tried to learn the name of the man Roosevelt wanted as his running mate. Hannegan decided the time had come to sap the Wallace strength and he gave the press a copy of the letter Roosevelt had written to Wallace. This was the weak letter in which the President said he would vote for Wallace if he were a delegate. The effect of the letter on the delegations was immediate, for nowhere had Roosevelt stated he wanted Wallace specifically for Vice-President.

On the following night Hannegan deflated the Byrnes balloon by giving the press copies of the "Harry Truman or Bill Douglas" letter Grace Tully had typed for him. Roosevelt's train was at San Diego and Byrnes put in a frantic telephone call to win a retraction. When Roosevelt refused to come to the phone, Byrnes realized that Hannegan had outwitted him. In great anger, he took the only course open to him, and this was to announce he was no longer a candidate.

On Wednesday, July 19, Roosevelt easily won renomination for a fourth term. The chief remaining question was the naming of the Vice-Presidential nominee. Hannegan, who suffered from high-blood pressure, was badly agitated because Henry Wallace had come to Chicago to direct his own campaign and was working hard to win the nomination.

On Thursday when the fight for the Vice-Presidency got underway on the convention floor, Hannegan turned paler when he learned that Truman was not acting as an active candidate. Out went a call to San Diego to inform the President that the fight had narrowed down to Wallace and Truman, but that Truman remained wary that the President wanted him.

Late that afternoon Truman was in a committee meeting when a messenger asked him to go immediately to Hannegan's suite. He sat on one of the twin beds while Hannegan sat on the other and telephoned Roosevelt. Roosevelt's normal telephone voice was so loud that it was necessary for Hannegan to told the receiver a foot from his ear. "Bob," Roosevelt yelled, "have you got that fellow lined up yet?"

"No," said Hannegan. "He is the contrariest Missouri mule I've ever dealt with."

"Well, you tell him," Truman heard the President shout, "if he wants to break up the Democratic Party in the midst of a war, that's his responsibility!" With that, Roosevelt hung up.

Afterward, Truman turned pale and said to Hannegan, "Why didn't he tell me in the first place?"

Even with Roosevelt's blessing, a major fight loomed because the Wallace forces were well organized. On the first ballot, Wallace did not get the necessary 589 votes, but for a while it seemed he would. His final total was 429½ to Truman's 319½.

Truman was sitting with the Missouri delegation in the hall and calmly munching a hot dog when the second ballot began. Wallace took an early lead, 148 to 125, and as the alphabetical call of the states continued, a see-saw battle developed. The vote stood 477½ for Truman and 472½ for Wallace when Hannegan decided the time had come to see if various state delegations were serious about their agreements to switch votes to Truman in exchange for government contracts for their states. At his signal, state after state changed their votes from Wallace to Truman. Cries of despair rose from the Wallace supporters long before Truman's total reached 1,031 votes.

The crowd now rushed to the Missouri delegation and carried him to the platform where Hannegan raised his arm. "I don't know what else I can say except that I accept this honor with all humility," Truman told the cheering convention. Back at Grandview, Martha Truman had listened to the convention on her radio. "I'm not a giggly woman," she told reporters, "but I can't help smiling when people cheer at the mention of Harry's name."

In August, Roosevelt returned to Washington from his meeting on strategy with Nimitz and MacArthur. He asked Truman to have lunch with him on August 17 and they ate on the White House South Grounds under a magnolia tree Andrew Jackson had planted. The President did not look well and requested Truman to campaign for both of them because he wanted to conserve his strength for running the war and planning the peace. Truman knew that reporters would ask him about Roosevelt's apppearance. Outside the White House he told them, "The President looked fine and ate a bigger meal than I did. He's keen as a briar."

Not long afterward, Truman went to a White House reception with Eddie McKim, his National Guard friend. When they left, McKim said to him, "Turn around and have a look. You're going to be living in that house before long."

"Eddie, I'm afraid I am," Truman replied. "And it scares the heck out of me."

Hannegan was concerned with Roosevelt's decision not to campaign, for he felt certain the Democrats would lose unless he did. He had no reason for his jitters, however, because Roosevelt was soon enraged by Republican insinuations regarding his health. Roosevelt called it "the meanest campaign of my life." So far as he was concerned, his poor health was only temporary and he fully expected to bounce back to his energetic condition of previous years. On September 23, he jumped into the campaign with a speech before the Teamsters Union in Washington. This was a speech that Republicans sadly agreed was his best political oration. Afterward, Hannegan quickly won his consent to five more speeches.

Truman was relieved that he would not have to carry the entire campaign load, for he realized that Roosevelt was without peer in an election fight. Nevertheless, he mapped out campaign trips that would carry him across the country and back. Although wealthy Democrats offered to pay all expenses for a costly campaign, he rejected the offer because he did not want to be indebted to them afterward. Instead, he traveled in the *Henry Stanley*, an old combination sleeping and club car, which was attached to any train traveling his route. In addition, he told the campaign funds committee to clear all contributions with him before acceptance.

Generally, Vice-Presidential candidates are ignored in campaigns, but Truman was much in the news that fall. *Time* magazine noted that "Anti-New Deal newspapers have examined the Truman record with the zeal of ballistic experts." Another magazine wrote, "The competence of Mr. Roosevelt's current running mate is the nearest thing the country has to a burning issue."

As he went from city to city, he found himself under attack because his wife was on his office payroll. He insisted she was well worth her salary. His former connections with

Tom Pendergast were given erroneous implications, and there were jeers because of the failure of his haberdashery store. There was also a widespread rumor that he was Jewish, to which he replied, "I am not Jewish but if I were I would not be ashamed of it."

A completely hostile audience in Los Angeles, he said, "threw more than a hundred pointed questions at me." In contrast, at a small town in Idaho, the entire audience turned out to be only three schoolteachers to whom he gave a fifteen-minute talk. In the state of Washington, he found that a "good candidate" was one who ate a heavy meal at every stop.

At Hyde Park, New York, on Tuseday evening, November 7, President Roosevelt sat at his dining room table, listening to election returns. Friends found him pessimistic, certain that Thomas E. Dewey, his Republican opponent, would defeat him.

An opposite scene was taking place at the Muehlebach Hotel in Kansas City. Here in the penthouse suite Truman was surrounded by Battery D buddies. When he noted their pessimism, he called out, "Everybody around here seems to be nervous but me." To lighten the atmosphere, he sat down at the piano and played Paderewski's *Minuet*.

Not until 3:45 A.M. did Dewey concede. By then the Democrats had won a resounding victory with 432 electoral votes to only 99 for the Republicans. "Three cheers for Captain Harry!" came the cry. However, it was Vice-President Truman's turn to grow serious now, for he realized that in the not-too-distant future he would become President of the United States.

16

---◆---

ROOSEVELT'S STANDBY

Aᴛᴛᴇʀ three hectic years running the Truman Committee, Truman was restless in the quiet chair of the Vice-President. He could not get used to his limited duties, which consisted of determining what Senate committee should receive an introduced bill and presiding over the Senate in session without taking part in debate. It was true he could cast a vote when the Senate was evenly divided on a bill, but this he knew from history was a rare event.

He had hoped to stretch his Constitutional straitjacket by taking on special assignments from the President. But hardly had both been sworn into office on January 20 when Roosevelt left Washington. He was on his way to the Yalta Conference in the Crimea to settle outstanding problems on the creation of the United Nations with Prime Minister Winston Churchill of Great Britain and dictator Joseph Stalin of the Soviet Union. There had been no time for a long conversation with the President and Truman's hope for added duties vanished. What remained for him were afternoons pounding a gavel in the Senate chamber and evenings given over to formal social functions.

Truman was Vice-President only six days when Tom Pendergast died. He had come out of prison penniless, broken in health and deserted by friends. It would have been politically wise for Truman to ignore the boss's passing because of the stir during the campaign about their connection. But Truman quickly boarded an Army bomber and flew to Kansas City. Although he was widely criticized afterward for attending the funeral, he boldly told reporters, "I'm as sorry as I can be. He was always my friend and I have always been his."

Exactly a month after Truman became Vice-President, a rumor swept the Capitol that Roosevelt was dead. Truman descended from his dais, his face ashen as he rushed to the office of Leslie L. Biffle, the Secretary of the Senate. He was too nervous to call the White House and he prevailed upon Biffle to telephone for him. With relief, Truman learned that the President was alive and on his way home from Yalta.

On March 1, Roosevelt came to the Capitol to give his report on the foreign conference to Congress and the nation. "He seemed a spent man. I had a hollow feeling within me," Truman admitted. Roosevelt spoke without his usual enthusiasm and the words came hard. He made the only public reference to his paralyzed legs when he apologized for sitting during his speech: "I know that you will realize it makes it a lot easier for me in not having to carry about ten pounds of steel around on the bottom of my legs."

During March, Truman saw Roosevelt only a few times and had no opportunity for a long conversation. When Roosevelt left for Warm Springs, Georgia, on March 30, to recuperate, his ill appearance was in sharp contrast to Truman's glowing health.

Yet shortly afterward the country almost lost its Vice-President. Although Truman did not enjoy fishing, he joined Speaker Rayburn and a few friends for some bass casting on an eastern Maryland lake. The boat suddenly lurched and Truman fell overboard into deep, cold water. When he was finally hauled into the boat, he sat shivering in a corner under a blanket. "You just go on and catch the fish, Sam," he called to worried Rayburn, "and I'll do the swimming."

Truman's eighty-second day as Vice-President came on April 12. That afternoon, while sitting at his desk facing the Senators, he wrote a letter to "Dear Mamma and Mary." In this letter he wrote: "Turn on your radio tomorrow night at 9:30 your time, and you'll hear Harry make a Jefferson Day address to the nation. It will be followed by the President, whom I'll introduce."

When the Senate recessed at 5:10, Truman headed for the House side of the Capitol for a meeting with Speaker Rayburn in his hideaway "Board of Education" room. He no sooner opened the door when Rayburn told him that the White House wanted him to call immediately. The switchboard operator connected him with Stephen Early, Roosevelt's press secretary. "Please come right over," Early said, in a choking voice. "And come through the main Pennsylvania entrance."

All the men in Rayburn's room watched Truman's face turn gray and his jaw set hard. "Holy General Jackson!" were his first words after he hung up. "Something must have happened."

He dashed out the door, ran the length of the Capitol basement and the underground tunnel leading to the Senate Office Building. After he picked up his hat, he ordered his government chauffeur to get his car.

It was 5:25 when he entered the White House and took

the elevator to the second floor, where he hurried to Mrs. Roosevelt's study. "Harry," Mrs. Roosevelt greeted him, pale but composed, "the President is dead."

Tears flowed down Truman's cheeks. "Is there anything I can do for you?" he stammered.

In a motherly fashion, she put a hand on his shoulder. "Tell us what we can do," she replied. "Is there any way we can help you?"

Mrs. Roosevelt said she wanted to go to Warm Springs and asked if she could use a government plane. Her request struck Truman as strange until he realized he was now President and she was a private citizen. "Of course, Mrs. Roosevelt," he told her.

In a daze, he got on the phone and called Biffle and Rayburn, requesting them to bring congressional leaders to the White House. Another call went to Chief Justice Harlan Stone to come immediately to swear him in. Then he called his apartment to break the news to his wife. Daughter Margaret answered the phone and he said bluntly, "Let me speak to your mother."

"Are you coming home to dinner?" she asked him.

"Margaret!" he yelled. "Will you let me speak to your mother!" Mrs. Truman burst into tears when she learned Roosevelt was dead. "Come right away with Margaret," he told her.

There was trouble finding a Bible when the Chief Justice arrived. Finally Roosevelt's Cabinet and the Truman family crowded into the Cabinet Room. The clock under Woodrow Wilson's portrait read 7:09 P.M. when Stone administered the oath to Truman. "Everyone was crying and carrying on," said Truman. "None of us could believe FDR was gone."

Least of all could Truman accustom himself to the position he now held—President of the United States.

17

ENDING WORLD WAR II

FEW Presidents entered office with greater crises facing the nation than did Harry Truman. The war was still on in Europe, though the end appeared in sight; in Asia, General MacArthur was retaking the Philippines and the gigantic task of subduing Japan lay yet ahead. In Eastern Europe, Stalin's Red armies were installing local Communist governments despite promises to the contrary made to Roosevelt at Yalta. The British and French governments were busily planning a return to their prewar empire status, despite the shouting demands of their colonies for self-government and independence. In China, the Nationalists under Chiang Kai-shek and the Communists under Mao Tse-tung were battling each other as well as the Japanese invaders. On the home front, the United States was a scene of much restlessness. Americans were tired of government controls, including the rationing of civilian goods and supplies, price and wage controls. There was also widespread concern that an end to military production would bring on serious unemployment and another depression.

In the midst of these problems, one of the most popular Presidents in American history lay dead and the general restlessness deepened because of concern regarding the new President's unknown views on domestic and foreign policy. People wondered what the new President's personality was and whether he could solve the massive problems facing them.

Roy Roberts, editor of the Kansas City *Star,* gave the nation its first interpretation of President Truman when he wrote: "Humility probably would be the first characterization. Then loyalty, common sense, deep patriotism, and above all an abiding faith in his country and its democratic system. . . . The sheer fact he is the average man, understands the average man and his quality, is probably Truman's greatest asset."

Truman's humility was borne out his first day when he went to the Capitol for lunch after a busy morning of briefings. On the way back to his oval White House office, he told reporters, "Boys, if you ever pray, pray for me now. I don't know whether you fellows ever had a load of hay fall on you, but when they told me yesterday what had happened, I felt like the moon, the stars and all the planets had fallen on me."

That afternoon he held more briefings and read a mountain of memos and reports that were delivered to his desk. He realized he had an enormous amount of background material to digest before he could make intelligent decisions. Yet momentous decisions had to be made from the start and in many cases he had to rely on his own native intelligence and reasoning powers rather than on full familiarity with each problem. That afternoon he learned much about the research on the atomic bomb and about Soviet intrigue in Eastern Europe. The UN was scheduled to begin meetings on April 25 in San Francisco to write that organization's charter and newspapers expressed concern that Truman would call it off. But he said he wanted it held on schedule. When he finally left his office at night, he carried with him a heavy briefcase filled with more memos and reports, all to be read before he returned again in the morning.

On Monday, April 16, came his first big test when he addressed Congress for the first time. He wrote his mother afterward, "It seemed to go over all right from the ovation I received." At Grandview, his ninety-two-year-old mother told reporters, "I can't really be glad he is President because I'm sorry that President Roosevelt is dead."

Day after day the military and diplomatic briefings continued, sandwiched between visits from officials from foreign governments and American agencies. Truman early revealed a frankness that startled those who expected vague and general talk from a new President. Once when Soviet Foreign Minister Molotov dropped in for a chat on his way to the UN Charter meeting at San Francisco, Truman berated him for establishing a Communist government in Poland after promising a free election there. Molotov stammered that no one had talked to him in a like manner in his entire life. "Carry out your agreements and you won't get talked to like that," Truman snapped.

At the outset, the Trumans lived in Blair House, the old square yellow government residence diagonally across Pennsylvania from the White House. He had told Mrs. Roosevelt to take her time about moving her possessions of thirteen years from the White House, and it was not until May 7 that the Trumans first occupied the upstairs living quarters of the White House. Early the next morning he wrote his mother regarding his double celebration. "I am sixty-one this morning and I slept in the President's room in the White House last night." Besides his birthday celebration, May 8 had even greater significance. This was V-E Day, victory in Europe with the unconditional surrender of the Germans.

One of Truman's early problems was that he had difficulty accustoming himself to his high status. "I never think of anyone as the President, but Mr. Roosevelt," he wrote the late President's widow. When former President Herbert Hoover called on him, Truman kept calling Hoover "Mr. President," to the latter's embarrassment. In turn, several government officials appointed by Roosevelt had trouble remembering that Truman was now President. Once Truman called an agency head and told him, "The President has sent John Snyder's name to the Senate for confirmation as Federal Loan Administrator."

The official asked, "Did the President make that appointment before he died?"

Truman's response was, "No— HE made it just now."

Truman realized that he needed his own selected Cabinet and close aides. He had asked Roosevelt's Cabinet to remain, even though he knew they were loyal to the dead President and not to him. It was only with great embarrassment that he finally requested resignations and made his own appointments. John Snyder became Secretary of the Treasury; Bob Hannegan, Postmaster General; his former Senate colleague, Louis Schwellenbach, Secretary of Labor; and Tom Clark, formerly of the Truman Committee staff, Attorney General. Ever since the 1944 convention, when Truman had won the

Vice-Presidential nomination, he had felt embarrassed about James Byrnes's loss to him in that fight. Because of this, he now named Byrnes as his Secretary of State.

Newsmen soon noticed that many Missourians were entering the government service. One paper wrote, "Battery D must have at least 10,000 men in it. They all want to see Truman." Harry Vaughan was now Brigadier General Vaughan and the President's military aide. Charlie Ross also went to work for his childhood friend, forsaking a career as a top Washington correspondent.

"Truman called me up and told me to come over to his office," Ross said. "When I walked in, his first words were, 'Charlie, I'm going to put your feet in the fire. I want you to come here and be my press secretary.'"

When Ross agreed, Truman placed a long-distance call to their old high school teacher, Miss Matilda Brown. "Miss Tillie," Truman told her, "I've just put Charlie in charge of my press relations."

"I started out by calling him Mr. President," Miss Tillie said later, "but went right back to calling him Harry." She asked Truman if he recalled graduation night when she kissed only Charlie Ross and told the others she hoped to kiss a future President of the United States.

During his first few months of office, Truman plunged into three vital efforts. The first was to establish the United Nations on a workable basis; the second, to bring about a peace treaty for postwar Europe; and the third, to force the unconditional surrender of Japan.

At San Francisco, the 1,100 delegates from 50 nations had hardly begun their task of writing the Charter, or constitution, for the proposed world organization when the Russians proved argumentative on almost every major paragraph.

Roosevelt had agreed at Yalta to give the Soviet Union three seats in the General Assembly, extra places for White Russia and the Ukraine. To keep the conference from collapsing, Truman had to agree to this prior arrangement. On the establishment of the Security Council, the Russians were insisting that a single veto could prevent the discussion of any dispute by the eleven-nation top body. Weeks of haggling finally ended when Truman cabled Harry Hopkins, his Moscow emissary, to insist that Stalin give in. Another long dispute arose because of Soviet opposition to granting the General Assembly free discussion of all topics and the right to make recommendations to the Security Council. When Truman threatened to go over Molotov's head directly to Stalin, the Soviet delegation finally agreed to make the General Assembly the "Town Meeting of the World."

Because of these arguments, the UN Charter Conference lasted two months before its basic document was ready for signing. Truman considered this such a momentous occasion that he went to San Francisco to address the final session on June 26, 1945. "Let us not fail to grasp this supreme chance to establish a worldwide rule of reason—to create an enduring peace under the guidance of God," he implored the delegates.

Afterward he flew to Missouri for the first time since becoming President. Enormous crowds were on hand when he arrived and wherever he went. "I can't be President in Jackson County," he told one large group. "I'm still county judge." He also dropped in for a visit with Eddie Jacobson at his new haberdashery store. When he ordered three white shirts size 15½–33, Jacobson was embarrassed. "I don't have any, Harry," he said. "You know, the war shortage. But I've got some red-hot bow ties." Truman spent several hours with his mother. Photographers kept snapping so many pictures that she finally said to her son, "If you're President, Harry, why can't you shoo all these people away?" Martha Truman had refused to let Secret Service men guard her home. "It isn't neighborly," she chided Truman. She had flown to Washington earlier to spend Mother's Day weekend with him and the crowds of reporters annoyed her. "Oh, fiddlesticks," she had greeted Truman at the airport, "why didn't you tell me there was going to be all this fuss and I wouldn't have come?"

When Truman returned to Washington from San Francisco, he made preparations for his second major task. To effect a European peace treaty and postwar territorial settlement, he and Secretary of State Byrnes went by boat to Europe on July 6 to meet with Stalin and Churchill at Potsdam, outside of war-shattered Berlin. Truman had asked General Eisenhower to arrange accommodations and conference space and these were in readiness when he arrived. Swarms of newsmen clustered around the three-story yellow mansion that housed Truman and the American delegation, and among the reporters was a young Bostonian named John F. Kennedy. Kennedy retired from the Navy because of injuries in April 1945.

Although Truman arrived on schedule, Churchill arrived a day late and Stalin did not come until July 17 because he was recuperating from a heart attack. Truman had not met either man before, yet when the conference began at five P.M. on the seventeenth, an informal atmosphere prevailed. Both Stalin and Churchill deferred to Truman to serve as presiding officer and he immediately announced a major four-part program: (1) to establish a Council of Foreign Ministers to develop the peace negotiations and territorial settlements;

(2) to create a Control Council for Germany to bring about her complete disarmament, eradicate Nazism and try war criminals; (3) free and unfettered elections in the liberated countries and in former enemy nations; (4) a generous peace with Italy and her early admission into the UN.

Between sessions the three leaders entertained each other at lavish affairs. Truman had requested pianist Eugene List to play a Chopin program, and it was not until afterward that he learned that Churchill had a dislike for classical music. Stalin also held a classical music evening and when it came Churchill's turn to entertain he had the British Royal Air Force Orchestra play loud military pieces.

Despite the informal atmosphere, Truman soon saw that the first meetings were not proving fruitful. Then on July 25, there was a fretful recess when Churchill returned to England because of the national election there. When the conference finally resumed at 10:15 p.m. on July 30, Clement Attlee held Churchill's place at the conference table, for his Labor Party had defeated Churchill's Conservative Party and he was now Prime Minister. The Potsdam Conference finally ended on August 2 with only a slight beginning toward reconverting Europe from war to peace. In a letter to his mother, Truman wrote, "I hope I never have to hold another conference with them [the Russians]."

It was at Potsdam that Truman undertook his third major effort. During the meetings word reached him of the successful explosion of an atomic bomb on July 16 at Alamogordo, New Mexico. Despite the air battering of Japan, that nation still had 2,500,000 soldiers on her islands and a million other soldiers in Manchuria. The Joint Chiefs of Staff had informed Truman that a military assault on the main island of Honshu, where Tokyo was located, would result in at least a half-million American casualties.

To Truman this was reason enough for dropping an atomic bomb on Japan. However, first he issued an ultimatum demanding that Japan surrender. This ultimatum was beamed by radio on a twenty-four hour basis to Japan and twenty-seven million leaflets were dropped on the enemy country. The official Japanese reply was that Truman's ultimatum was "absurd." Next Truman polled 150 American scientists who had worked on the bomb and 90 percent urged him to use it.

The final decision was Truman's alone. "I wanted to save a half-million boys on our side and as many on the other side," he explained his order, which led to the dropping of A-bombs on Hiroshima and Nagasaki.

The horror wrought by the bombs brought about the surrender of Japan on August 14, after that country won Truman's assurance that Emperor Hirohito would remain in office. World War II was now at an end, with the formal surrender of the Japanese on the battleship *Missouri* in Tokyo Bay on September 2, 1945.

18

POSTWAR PROBLEMS

Despite the wild national rejoicing on V-J Day, Truman realized that a dangerous road stretched ahead to secure the peace and make way for a more democratic world. The United States had emerged from the war as the strongest power on earth, and Truman knew that only a humane and responsible leadership would help the less fortunate nations recover from the ravages of war. This meant American economic aid to the weakened powers in Europe and Asia plus a continual prodding to raise standards of living, end colonialism and strengthen civil rights. Standing directly in the path of these goals was the Soviet Union, intent upon world conquest and the spread of Communism.

Basic to American leadership was the necessity for the United States to maintain and increase her own economic strength. To Truman's way of thinking, the country must not falter at this crucial hour. Noted economists were already gloomily predicting that the country would soon be plunged into another major depression with at least eight million unemployed. In addition, isolationists were emerging from wartime silence to resume their call for a return to the principle of no foreign entanglements.

Only four days after V-J Day, Truman took his first major step by sending Congress a 21-point program, calling for an "Economic Bill of Rights." He asked Congress to pass legislation to promote full employment, increase minimum wages, extend unemployment compensation, increase farm income, set up private and public housing programs, a national health program, aid to education, increased Social Security payments, power development programs similar to the Tennessee Valley Authority and a permanent Fair Employment Practices Committee to provide equal job opportunities regardless of race or religion.

It was this program that was to end his "honeymoon" with Congress and bring on a struggle that lasted as long as he was President. Opponents did their best to promote a personal campaign of ridicule against him, and he soon found himself referred to as "a little man" and "bewildered" both in Congress and in the press.

Truman paid little attention to these personal attacks. "I have never cared about all the lies that were said about me as long as I knew what I was doing was right," he said. However, he grew furious when his wife and daughter were attacked. "There is no reason to malign the women in the White House," he insisted. "The attacks made on Mrs. Truman were almost as bad as those made on the two most maligned women in the White House, Mrs. Lincoln and Mrs. Franklin Roosevelt."

Not long after Truman unveiled his 21-point program, he found that almost every subject he handled became laden with controversy. When he fired Secretary of the Interior Harold Ickes, who refused to support him, many Roosevelt supporters labeled Truman falsely as an enemy of the late President's principles. When he was photographed wearing a sport shirt on vacation, grinning, joking or speaking in his frank manner, columnists declared him to be without culture. Personal criticism grew so great that at one point Truman sat down and wrote a memo to himself.

In this memo, he said he needed four new Kitchen Cabinet Secretaries. The first would be the Secretary of Inflation, with the job of convincing people that no matter how high prices rose or how low wages fell, no real problem existed. The second Secretary would be the Secretary of Reaction, to abolish "flying machines" and "restore oxcarts, oar boats and sailing ships." The third would function as the Secretary of Columnists, to read all columns so he could "run the United States and the world as it should be." The last would be the Secretary of Semantics to supply him with "40- to 50-dollar words." This Secretary would also advise him how to remain silent while talking at the same time and would put him in favor of inflation in one city and against it in another.

By late fall of 1945, his burdens grew more complex because so many issues had to be handled at the same time. For instance, a great national issue had arisen regarding the future of the atomic bomb and nuclear energy. Many Congressmen and editors were demanding that further developments in this field be made an exclusive function of the military branch of the government. This brought on an immediate public frenzy. At first, Truman stayed out of the controversy, but finally he decided that civilian and not military control was in the American tradition. The fight lasted until mid-1946, when Congress established the civilian Atomic Energy Commission. At the same time, the decision as to the military use of the bomb was made the exclusive right of the President.

Another major problem was the growing animosity between labor and management. Strikes had broken out in the oil, lumber, aircraft, meat-packing, aluminum, automobile and steel industries. A single strike call by the United Auto Workers had idled 175,000 men in 19 states. Truman considered these strikes not only damaging to the continuation of a smooth-running economy but also a threat to rehabilitation work abroad. When Congress refused to honor his request for a law to establish fact-finding boards to investigate each labor dispute, Truman went ahead and did this on his own. His first fact-finding board recommended an $18\frac{1}{2}\mathcal{c}$ an hour wage increase in the steel industry, and when steel companies accepted this other industries quickly agreed to accept this formula for settling their disputes.

However, just when it appeared that Truman had easily solved the strike problem, two of the Railroad Brotherhoods refused to abide by the formula. Angrily, Truman called Alvanley Johnson, head of the Locomotive Engineers, and Alexander Whitney, of the Railroad Trainmen, to the White House for a frank talk. These were the men who had helped Truman in his 1940 reelection fight, yet their current threat of a major strike strained their friendship. "If you think I'm going to sit here and let you tie up this country, you're crazy," Truman warned them. "I am going to protect the public and we are going to run these railroads!"

The two postponed their strike call five days, but when they finally called it Truman was outraged. First he addressed the nation by radio and denounced the two as "men who place their private interests above the welfare of the nation." Then the next afternoon he rode to the Capitol and told Congress, "I request the Congress immediately to authorize the President to draft into the armed forces all workers who are on strike against the government." Just as he finished his statement, Secretary of the Senate Biffle tugged on his arm and told him Whitney and Johnson had called off their strike.

There was yet another major labor controversy and this was with John L. Lewis, head of the United Mine Workers. After a seven-week strike with a loss of 90,000,000 tons of coal desperately needed by American industry and European countries, Truman ordered the Department of the Interior to take over the mines in May 1946. For a few months the government ran the mines, then Lewis called a strike against the government. This time Truman ordered legal action, and a federal court fined Lewis $10,000 and the UMW, $3,500,000. After Lewis's strike was broken, he called Truman "a malignant scheming sort of an individual and a man totally unfitted for the position."

Despite his vexing domestic problems, Truman concentrated much of his effort on foreign policy. By personal decisions he prevented France from annexing part of Italy and regaining colonial domination over Syria and Lebanon. He also let Marshal Tito, the territorial-hungry Communist dictator of Yugoslavia, know that if he attempted to seize Trieste, the United States would use force to oust him. "I did the same thing with Stalin," said Truman, "when he was threatening to settle his forces down for good in Iran. I ordered the Mediterranean Fleet into the Persian Gulf and told Stalin he had better get out before they got there. And he did, too."

A great deal of confusion remained among Americans whether to consider World War II Soviet allies postwar friends or foes. Truman moved the country to a greater realization of the U.S.S.R.'s postwar ambitions when he accompanied former British Prime Minister Winston Churchill to Westminster College in Missouri, where Churchill was to speak on March 5, 1946. After Truman introduced him with these words, "I know he will say something constructive," Churchill made his speech in which he said, "From Stettin in the Baltic to Trieste in the Adriatic, an iron curtain has descended across the continent. From what I have seen of our Russian friends and Allies during the war, I am convinced that there is nothing they admire so much as strength, and there is nothing for which they have less respect than for military weakness."

By the time Truman returned to Washington, he found that most Americans agreed with Churchill's "Iron Curtain" speech. However, a strong and noisy minority clamored for soft treatment of the Communists and blamed the United States for forcing Stalin to take belligerent action around the globe. The leader of this point of view was Secretary of Commerce Henry Wallace, whom Truman had defeated for the Vice-Presidency in 1944.

At first, Truman ignored Wallace's statements and memos regarding American-Soviet relations. But the issue between the two men came to a head on September 10, 1946, when Wallace came to the White House with copies of a speech he was to deliver in New York on the twelfth. Wallace later claimed that Truman read through his speech and approved it. Truman, however, insisted that he did not read it but merely thumbed through it.

In truth, much of Wallace's speech attacked Soviet activities. But on the other hand, he also declared that "Russia must be convinced that we are not planning war against her." This gave the impression that Truman was misunderstanding Russia's position and the speech, therefore, caused great consternation among the anti-Communist allies of the United States.

On September 20, Truman phoned Wallace and said, "Henry, I'm sorry but I have reached the conclusion that it will be best if I ask for your resignation." And with the departure of Wallace went all remaining doubts about the direction of the foreign policy of the United States.

Even though Truman had rid himself of Wallace, taken strong action against Stalin's first postwar maneuvers and worked overtime to keep the American economy running at a high pace, by the fall of 1946 his popularity was at a low point. Shortly after he had succeeded Roosevelt, the Gallup Poll reported that 87 percent of the population favored him, but now only 32 percent did.

This dive in popularity was borne out in the congressional elections in November 1946 when the Republicans won control of the next, or 80th Congress. The personal attacks on him now broadened, and as one Republican summed up the 80th Congress, "Congress opened daily with a prayer and ended with a probe."

Although Truman relentlessly continued to press this antagonistic Congress for action on his 21-point program, his failures with this new Congress exceeded those with the preceding Congress. Not only did the 80th Congress ignore his domestic program but it defied Truman by passing legislation he opposed. When he vetoed its tax bill, it easily mustered the necessary two-thirds vote to pass it over the veto.

It was on labor legislation that the 80th Congress revealed

its chief independence from White House control. President Roosevelt had won from Congress the National Labor Relations Act, which gave organized labor the government's sanction to establish unions throughout American industry. Truman believed in the necessity of strong unions to bargain on fair terms with management. However, he had witnessed the wartime development of "Big Labor," which was so strong that a strike call could paralyze large segments of industry.

To decrease the power of irresponsible union leaders, Truman requested Congress to provide for a 30-day "cooling-off" period when a strike threatened. He also asked for a law abolishing jurisdictional strikes, or strikes brought on by competing unions who wanted to represent workers in a plant or industry.

But Congress went much further than his proposals by passing the Taft-Hartley Act in June 1947. This act outlawed industry-wide strikes, mass picketing and the closed shop where only union members could be employed. In addition, it established "cooling-off" periods, prohibited the use of union funds for political contributions, required union leaders to file non-Communist affidavits and gave the President authority to get court injunctions barring strikes for eighty days in industries involving interstate commerce, public utilities and communications.

Truman denounced the Taft-Hartley Bill as a "slave labor act," and promptly vetoed it. But just as promptly, Congress passed it over his veto.

On noneconomic issues, Congress proved less contrary. It passed his proposals to unify the armed services into a Department of Defense, to establish the Central Intelligence Agency, to authorize his Hoover Commission to study gov-

ernment operations and recommend ways to improve efficiency and to establish a new line of presidential succession
so that the House Speaker was next in line behind the Vice-
President and not the Secretary of State.

Truman's chief successes with the 80th Congress were in
foreign relations, a field that proved a constant headache.
Shortly after the Congress convened, Prime Minister Attlee
informed Truman that Britain could no longer continue its
financial and military aid to Greece. In 1944, when the Nazis
were driven from Greece, the British had entered that dev-
astated land with an army of 40,000 and economic aid. But
civil war promoted by Communist Greek rebels kept that
ancient land in constant turmoil. In addition, the Communist governments of Yugoslavia, Albania and Bulgaria threatened to come to the aid of the Greek Communists.

Several members of Truman's Cabinet argued against step-
ping into the Greek troubles. But Truman realized that if
the United States did not act, the Soviet Government would
fill the vacuum after the British departed. Moreover, the
U.S.S.R. was pressing Greece's neighbor Turkey for territorial concessions and special privileges to permit the Russian navy free access into the Mediterranean. Turkey was
already on the point of bankruptcy because of her necessity
to maintain an army of 600,000 soldiers. Soviet victories in
Turkey and Greece would seriously damage the American
image throughout the world. Even worse, such events would
bring despair to other nations beset by Communists from
within and by Soviet threats from without.

A grim-faced Truman rode up Pennsylvania Avenue to
the Capitol on March 12, 1947, to propose a major change
in American foreign policy. "I believe it must be the policy
of the United States to support free peoples who are resist-

ing attempted subjugation by armed minorities or by outside pressures," he told Congress. "I believe that we must assist free peoples to work out their own destinies in their own way. The United Nations are not in a position to extend help of the kind that is required."

There was an immediate, strong outcry from many groups against the "Truman Doctrine." Some said that the United States could not afford the expense; others, that Greece and Turkey were not democracies, that the Truman Doctrine would weaken the infant UN, that it would result in war with the U.S.S.R. But the Truman Doctrine passed Congress, and with an initial appropriation of $250 million for Greek aid and $150 million for Turkish aid, both countries were saved from Communism.

The Truman Doctrine had set Truman and his advisers to thinking further about American foreign policy. Europe had failed to recover from the ravages of war. Britain had almost gone under because of a severe financial crisis in 1945 and only an American loan of $3,750,000,000 had temporarily eased her troubles. The entire European continent was like a feeble old man by 1947, tired and weak and unable to provide for himself.

Truman noted that with this condition prevailing, the Russians "were coldly determined to exploit the helpless condition of Europe to further Communism." European economies could not possibly revive without strong outside aid, and the United States must lend a generous hand before it was too late.

Truman had accepted an invitation to speak at the Delta Council at Cleveland, Mississippi, on May 8, 1947. For this occasion, he and his aides prepared an address that would be a blueprint of a plan to revitalize and rehabilitate the

European economy. However, Truman's ninety-four-year-old mother was seriously ill at that time and he turned over his speech to Under Secretary of State Dean G. Acheson. It was Acheson who therefore made the first appeal for the proposal that later became known as the Marshall Plan. "The war will not be over," said Acheson, "until the people of the world can again feed and clothe themselves and face the future with some degree of confidence. Free peoples who are seeking to preserve their independence and democratic institutions and human freedoms against totalitarian pressures will receive top priority for American reconstruction."

In January 1947, Truman had fired Secretary of State Byrnes because he found that Byrnes had wanted to run the State Department without any interference from the White House. He had replaced Byrnes with General George Marshall, former Army Chief of Staff. Now less than a month after Acheson's speech, Marshall again publicized Truman's proposal at the Harvard commencement exercises on June 5.

While Acheson's speech had gained little public attention, Marshall's Harvard address evoked international response. European nations sent delegates to Paris to discuss what American aid they would need to emerge from their economic doldrums. Then the State Department examined the figures and Truman sent Congress his Marshall Plan proposal, calling for a total of $17,000,000,000 in American aid over the next four years. When the Marshall Plan passed Congress after a bitter series of debates, Truman had what he wanted—a program of economic rehabilitation for the Western European nations as a bulwark against Communism.

It was during the initial determination of the Marshall Plan that Truman suffered a personal loss. On the morning of July 26, he learned that his mother was rapidly failing. At noon he boarded the Presidential plane, the *Independence,* for home. An hour along the ride to Grandview his pilot received word that Martha Truman was dead. "Well, now she won't have to suffer any more," Truman said chokingly. As his plane continued west, he composed a short biography of his mother. Later he cried unashamed when she was buried next to his father, dead since 1914.

Truman had other successes in foreign policy during this period. With Latin America he tried the personal approach. For instance, in the spring of 1947, he visited Mexico, a country long suspicious of her northern neighbor. Perhaps the single gesture that won Mexico over to Truman was his impromptu visit to Chapultepec Castle. Here a century before when General Winfield Scott's U.S. soldiers stormed the heights and took the castle, which was Mexico's West Point, the sole six cadet survivors inside committed suicide rather than surrender. With deep emotion Truman walked to the impressive monument to Los Niños Heroes, placed a wreath there and bowed his head. The cadets who were standing guard burst into tears at Truman's display. "I know the history of this incident," Truman said. "Brave men do not belong to any one country. I respect bravery wherever I see it." His words, widely quoted, brought national "vivas" below the Rio Grande.

Truman journeyed on another "good neighbor" trip to Rio de Janeiro in August 1947. Here twenty Western Hemisphere nations were meeting to write a mutual assistance pact to prevent future wars within the Americas. Their final agreement said that when any aggression occurred on an American nation, whether by an outside nation or by one of the twenty signing nations, the other member nations would be obligated to take action against the culprit. More than a million persons lined the Rio Branca to cheer "Señor Missouri" when Truman arrived to sign the pact. As in Mexico, he won tremendous good will by his simplicity and friendliness.

One of Truman's most difficult foreign problems during this period was the fate of Palestine. The Holy Land had been under British mandate since the close of World War I. The Balfour Declaration of 1917 had promised Palestine as a Jewish homeland, and Truman believed it should now be honored. In view of the plight of European Jewish refugees after World War II, Truman announced shortly after the Potsdam Conference, "The American view on Palestine is that we want to let as many Jews into Palestine as is possible to let into that country. Then the matter will have to be worked out diplomatically with the British and the Arabs, so that if a state is set up they may be able to set it up on a peaceful basis."

The British White Paper of 1939 limited the number of certificates of entry by Jews into Palestine. By late 1945 all the certificates had been used and Truman wrote Attlee asking that Britain grant an additional 100,000 certificates to Jewish refugees in Germany and Austria. "No other single matter is so important," he wrote, "for those who have known the horrors of concentration camps for over a decade as is the future of immigration possibilities into Palestine."

However, instead of acting on Truman's proposal, Attlee established a Joint Anglo-American Committee of Inquiry to hold hearings to determine where to settle Europe's up-rooted Jews. When this committee finally recommended an additional 100,000 certificates the following April, Attlee refused to honor it. His course of action was to arm the Arabs of Palestine and this in turn brought on violence by Jewish terrorists there.

Truman now found himself denounced by all sides. The British Government claimed he was meddling in an affair that did not concern the United States; Arabs insisted that Palestine was theirs and not a subject for discussion; and Jewish Zionists said that Truman's approval of the Joint Committee's organization in the first place showed that he was willing to participate in delaying tactics. In addition, Truman found that several officials in his own State Department were working against his policy of establishing a Jewish homeland.

Despite all the boiling animosities, Truman suggested that Attlee join with the United States in another effort to find a solution. This time a Joint Cabinet Committee met in London in July 1946 and recommended that Palestine be partitioned into Jewish and Arab zones and a separate central government zone covering Jerusalem, Bethlehem and the Negev. The native zones would be governed by Jews and Arabs selected by the British while the central zone would be completely British.

Truman immediately rejected this recommendation. When all sides heaped criticism on him for varying reasons, he said, "I surely wish God Almighty would have given the Children of Israel an Isaiah, the Christians a St. Paul and the Sons of Ishmael a peep at the Golden Rule."

In 1947, the British Government dumped the Palestine problem into the lap of the UN and Foreign Minister Ernest Bevin charged that Truman had "spoiled my plans" with his suggestions.

Throughout 1947, the United Nations Special Committee on Palestine studied the problem. In the fall it recommended separate Jewish and Arab states with Jerusalem remaining under UN trusteeship. Then in November the UN General Assembly approved the partition plan by a vote of 33 to 13. This solution seemed fair to Truman, though on March 19, Warren Austin, his representative to the UN Security Council, acted on his own and declared that the United States did not favor partition.

This immediately provoked consternation in the ranks of the Zionists who believed that Truman had broken his pledge for a Jewish homeland. Nevertheless, on May 14, 1948, with the British announcement of a pull-out from Palestine the next day, Truman recognized the Jewish Provisional Government of Israel as the legitimate government in that area.

The aftermath was war between the Arabs and Jews. But the new nation that Truman had worked so hard to establish held its own and remained in existence.

So while Truman met with little success in domestic legislation, in foreign affairs he revealed a courageous and creative leadership.

19

---◆---

THE 1948 CAMPAIGN

Eᴀʀʟʏ in 1948, Democratic Party leaders began their consideration of that year's Presidential election. From their examination of opinions from the various sections of the country, they came to a hurried conclusion that the party could not win in November if President Truman were their candidate.

First of all, Henry Wallace had announced the formation of a third party, the Progressive Party, and they feared that many former Roosevelt New Dealers would enter his camp if Truman ran. Then there were the important labor leaders who publicly asserted they would not endorse Truman for another four years in the White House. Dan Tobin, head of the Teamsters Union, who had been close to Roosevelt, went so far as to refer to Truman as "that squeaky-voice tinhorn."

Third, Truman had alienated Southern Democrats and endangered the "Solid South" vote for the party when he sent Congress a strong civil rights program in February 1948.

In this message, he called for an end to Jim Crow laws on trains and buses running between states, the protection of each citizen's right to vote, a federal law against lynching and a national Fair Employment Practices Committee to insure equal job treatment for minorities. When a Democratic National Committeewoman from Alabama complained personally to Truman about his civil rights program, he read the Bill of Rights to her and said, "I'm everybody's President. I take back nothing of what I propose and make no excuse for it."

There were in addition other events that produced head-shaking among party leaders. Individuals in the Administration were involved in speculation on the grain market and many newspapers headlined the wrongdoings, placing blame on Truman personally.

Then there was the subject of "Truman's balcony," which he ordered built off his second floor study. Even though he pointed out that Jefferson, who had designed the White House's south portico, intended there be a balcony, newspapers denounced him for making an addition to the Executive Mansion. One New York paper charged that he had "a lamentable penchant for meddling with a historic structure which the nation prefers as it is." Truman's reply was that "all changes in the White House since Fillmore's time have faced resistance—like gas lights and cooking stoves."

Assessing all these deficits to Truman's candidacy, several state chairmen, city bosses, three of President Roosevelt's sons, labor leaders and Southern Congressmen decided to promote another candidate. And the man they selected was popular General Eisenhower, who had left the government after serving Truman as Army Chief of Staff and now held the presidency of Columbia University.

There was a question whether Eisenhower was a Democrat or a Republican, and the general would not say. In January he had asked to have his name removed from the New Hampshire Republican Presidential primary, expressing his belief that "lifelong professional soldiers should abstain from seeking high political office." Democrats strangely took his withdrawal from the Republican primary to mean that he was doing so because he was a Democrat.

As a result, the "Ike Boom" among Democrats ballooned. When he did not publicly reject their offers of support, Truman's opposers rejoiced that his cause appeared doomed.

Truman's friends were convinced that the path to the nomination by the Democratic National Convention lay on top a steep mountain. It was important that he show the lesser party leaders that he could arouse popular enthusiasm. But how could he do this when he was a notoriously poor speaker?

Charlie Ross said, "One of our major concerns was that when he made a speech he sounded lifeless and uninspired and was always racing for the period. But a change came abruptly when he spoke to the American Society of Newspaper Editors in Washington. He gave a dull, prepared radio address, and there was little audience enthusiasm. But when he was off the air, he didn't sit down. Instead he launched into an extemporaneous off-the-record talk on national problems. The language was entirely his own, earthy and warm, and the audience went wild." Several editors told Ross afterward, "If Truman campaigned that way, he'd be hard to beat."

It was Truman's intention to talk just that way to the people across the nation. But he faced the stumbling block of an empty Democratic treasury. The answer to his dilemma came when the University of California asked him to accept an honorary degree and speak at its commencement exercises. Since a trip across the country to California would be nonpolitical he could charge expenses to the Presidential travel allowance, and he promptly accepted.

On June 3, when his 18-car train was ready for the long journey to the Pacific, he told reporters, "If I felt any better, I couldn't stand it." Out across the country the train moved slowly, making frequent stops for his off-the-cuff rear platform talks. Newsmen were surprised at his warm reception everywhere. This was a new Truman, an easy speaker who evoked loud cheers from trainyard audiences. He hit at the 80th Congress for not legislating his domestic program and without embarrassment he went into the prolonged campaign of editor opponents to make him out to be a fool. "They've been telling you a lot of things about your President, that he doesn't know what goes on, that he can't handle the government . . . about my ability or inability, my intelligence or lack of it."

In Chicago, 100,000 persons lined the streets to greet him, and in Omaha he strutted eight blocks with his old Battery D buddies in the 35th Division's annual parade. At Berkeley, where he was presented with an honorary degree, 50,000 turned out to hear his excellent address on foreign policy. At Albuquerque, where he labeled the 80th Congress as the "worst Congress," an excited listener interrupted him by yelling, "Lay it on, Harry! Give 'em hell!" Truman paused momentarily. "I will! I intend to!" he called back. "There is just one issue—the special interests against the people."

On June 18 he was back in Washington, in time for the adjournment of the Congress. Before it quit, it showed its power over him by passing three bills over his vetoes. Republican Congressmen denounced his "nonpolitical" trip as being full of politics. Opposing editors said he had made "a spectacle of himself that would reflect dishonorably on a ward heeler." Senator Robert Taft denounced him for "blackguarding Congress at every whistle stop." Taft was soon sorry for his words for he was deluged with telegrams from irate mayors who denied that their cities were "whistle stops."

On June 24, the day the Republican National Convention nominated New York's Governor Thomas E. Dewey for President, Truman had to lay politics aside. The problem that had suddenly arisen was Berlin.

On June 18, Truman had ordered currency reforms in the American zone of occupation. He had done so because the Soviet Government had obtained American occupation paper money-making plates. While the United States, France and Britain attempted to produce only enough money to match the quantity of goods and services produced in their zones of occupation, the U.S.S.R. was flooding Western Germany with so many American occupation "greenbacks" that a severe inflation threatened to result.

On June 24, only six days after Truman ordered the change in money plates, the Soviet Union retaliated, sealing off all access between Western occupation zones and Berlin, deep within the Soviet zone. The United States had made an oral agreement with the Soviet Union in 1945, to insure free access to the former German capital, which was to be administered by the United States, Britain, France and the U.S.S.R. But now came an arrogant message from Moscow denying the right of the Western powers to be in Berlin.

At a hastily assembled White House meeting, some of Truman's advisers questioned whether the United States should

stay in Berlin. "We are going to stay. Period!" Truman said.
Secretary of Defense James Forrestal proposed using armored
trains to keep contact open with the beleaguered city of
2,400,000 persons. Others favored a preventive war with
atomic bombs dropped on Moscow, and still others proposed
ending diplomatic relations with the Soviet Union. Truman
rejected all these proposals. "As long as the Russians are
willing to continue talks—however futile—there will be no
shooting," he said.

He was aware, however, that talks would not keep Ber-
liners alive. Unless supplies continued to arrive there, starvation would soon follow. With the railroad line and the highways blocked, there remained only one way to reach Berlin.
On June 26, Truman ordered all planes in the American
European Command to deliver food, clothing and fuel to
Berlin until the Soviet Union backed down. General Hoyt
Vandenberg of the Air Force complained that this was too
dangerous an undertaking, but Truman refused to accept
his argument.

Truman's bold decision paid off. The Berlin Airlift was
to last until May 12, 1949, when the Russians ended the land
blockade. Said Senator Tom Connally, chairman of the Senate Foreign Relations Committee, "It was a dangerous feat
but in the end it paid off. The Soviets held us in higher
esteem and the non-Communist European countries knew
they could count on us."

While Truman was busy with the Berlin crisis, Democratic
leaders were completing arrangements for their National
Convention, which was to begin on July 12 in Philadelphia.
Despite Truman's successful springtime whistle-stop tour,
party bosses continued to beseech General Eisenhower to accept the Presidential nomination. Boss after boss visited him

on the campus of Columbia University before he took himself out of contention on July 5 with this statement, "I will
not at this time identify myself with any political party and
could not accept nomination for any political office."

Had Eisenhower issued this statement earlier, the bosses
might have had time to build up another candidate for the
nomination. The result was that Truman's nomination was
now a foregone conclusion, and when the Convention opened
an air of defeat hung over the gathering. The delegates were
aware that not a single columnist or polltaker gave Truman
any chance of defeating Dewey.

All this defeatism showed up in the long faces of the delegates and in the sleepwalking pace of the proceedings. Everything seemed to go wrong. When taps sounded for the war
dead, the bugler hit several wrong notes. Then when opera
singer Lawrence Tibbett sang the "Star Spangled Banner,"
the organist gave him such a high pitch that he sounded as
though he were strangling. There was a further shock when
the Convention adopted a strong civil rights plank in the
platform. Thirty-five Southern delegates quit the Convention and organized their own political party, nominating
Governor J. Strom Thurmond of South Carolina for President. "We will never vote Republican, never vote for Truman and never accept the civil rights program," a spokesman
said.

Late in the afternoon of the fourteenth, Truman went to
Philadelphia to accept the nomination in person. It was
two A.M. when the delegates finished their listless balloting
and nominated Truman for President and Senator Alben
Barkley for Vice-President. Truman had asked Justice William Douglas of the Supreme Court to be his running mate
but Douglas had rejected the offer.

Banners carrying the slogan "We're Just Mild About Harry" greeted Truman when he stepped to the platform. Fifty doves had been released to brighten his entrance but several fell dead from heat exhaustion. One live dove perched on House Speaker Sam Rayburn's head as he greeted Truman on the platform.

Barkley spoke first and his short acceptance speech drew little applause from the weary delegates. Then came Truman. He stared out into the sea of exhausted and sour faces and he called out, "Senator Barkley and I will win this election and make these Republicans like it—don't you forget that!" The delegates stirred at Truman's fighting mood and they rose to their feet with wild cheers.

For twenty minutes before that dawn Truman spoke in the language of the man on the whistle-stop tour and the Convention was alive with enthusiasm for the first time. Delegates cheered his attacks on the 80th Congress for its failure to act on his domestic program and they screamed in delight when he said, "On the twenty-sixth of July, which out in Missouri we call 'Turnip Day,' I am going to call Congress back and ask them to pass laws to halt rising prices, to meet the housing crisis."

When he left the platform, it was to resounding applause. He had come an unwanted man. He left as a leader.

The Turnip Day Special Session of Congress lasted only two weeks, too short a time to act on legislation. When it finally adjourned, Truman had more ammunition to turn on the 80th Congress.

Yet despite the momentary excitement Truman had brought to the Democratic Convention and the inactivity of the Special Session, he had little reason to believe he could win the national election. First, Governor Dewey was acknowledgedly a strong campaigner and his campaign was backstopped by wealthy supporters. Second, the Democrats were now splintered into three factions: the regular Democrats behind Truman; the Progressive Party with Wallace; and the States' Rights Party with Governor Thurmond.

As a result, the Gallup, Crossley and Roper polls quickly concluded that Dewey would win overwhelmingly. One distinguished columnist said that Truman would be so badly defeated that the Democratic Party would cease to exist as a national political force. Indeed, several of Truman's Cabinet members and sub-Cabinet officers took this to heart and quietly let it be known their houses would be up for sale the following January.

As Truman prepared to start his campaign, he learned that the Democratic treasury was unable to meet expenses. Letters and phone calls for money to prominent Democrats by the National Committee went unanswered. The situation appeared hopeless until Louis A. Johnson, former Assistant Secretary of War, agreed to take over the fund-raising job. At the outset he met expenses by paying bills from his own pocket. If he had not done so the campaign could not have got under way.

The lack of money and the splintering of the Democratic Party were not all of Truman's problems. Favorable newspaper publicity would have gone a long way to help his cause. But Truman found that only 20 percent of the nation's papers with a mere 10 percent of daily circulation were on his side.

Truman realized he was embarking on a lonely venture. But he did his best under such circumstances, said General Vaughan. "He got his baptism in 1940 when he was all alone in that campaign, deserted by his so-called friends."

In August, Secretary of the Senate Biffle wandered through-out several states in old clothes to do some polling on his own among farmers and workers. After three weeks he re-turned to Washington and told Truman, "I think you can win." Truman stared at him with disbelief and asked, "Do you really think so, Les?"

In September the campaign began with the Republicans violating the first principle of a successful campaign by laugh-ing publicly at Truman's candidacy. "I want to see the peo-ple," Truman angrily told Charlie Ross. "I'm going to visit every whistle stop in the United States."

He started first with a six-speech day in Michigan on Labor Day. Despite a pouring rain, the crowds were enormous and greeted him enthusiastically. "We are in a hard and tough fight against shrewd and rich opponents." He shook a fist. "They know they can't count on your vote. Their only hope is that you won't vote at all. They have misjudged you."

On September 17, Barkley and General Marshall were at Union Station in Washington to see him off on a cross-country swing. "Mow 'em down!" Barkley begged him. Tru-man assured him he would.

Across the country traveled the Presidential train, the *Ferdinand Magellan,* a reconstructed armor-plated Pullman sold to the government for $1 in 1942. At Dexter, Iowa, he spoke to 75,000 farmers at the national plowing contest and they cheered him as he told stories about his own ten years as a Missouri farmer. "I can plow a straight furrow," he said. "A prejudiced witness said so—my mother."

Dewey also spoke in Iowa, traveling there almost at the same time as Truman. He spoke to a much smaller crowd, but reporters called his campaign debut "opulent" and Tru-man's "threadbare and visibly unsuccessful."

Truman's campaign trip was to be a 21,928-mile venture, the longest land campaign tour in history. Before it was finished, he talked to about 15 million people, giving 275 prepared speeches and, as he put it "about 200 more off the record." On one day he made 16 speeches.

At first, the Truman campaign ran amateurishly and the Republicans more than ever considered his effort a joke. But as the *Magellan* rolled on toward California, the campaign slowly became more organized. Under Secretary of the Interior Oscar Chapman worked up data sheets informing Truman where he would be stopping en route, the names of local dignitaries who would board the train and the significant features to mention about each community. At each stop two of Truman's aides jumped off the train, mingled with the crowd and led the applause at the proper time.

After a while the routine grew standardized. At each stop the local high school band blared out "Hail to the Chief." Then came the presentation of a gift to Truman, his modest thank you, a welcome to local Democratic leaders and compliments to the community for local achievements. After these came Truman's talk attacking the 80th Congress— "That Congress never did anything the whole time it was in session." He would also speak about his program and what he hoped to accomplish if he were elected.

After his political talk, he asked the crowd if it would like to meet his family. When Mrs. Truman appeared on the back platform, he identified her as "the boss." Then he brought out daughter Margaret and introduced her as "my baby" and "the boss's boss." These introductions proved to be the hit of each stop.

Secret Service men were concerned when he climbed off the train to shake hands with his listeners. Once Truman noticed a cowboy on a skittish horse ride through the crowd to the rear platform. Truman saw that the nervous horse might harm those about him, so he slowly climbed off the platform and grasped the horse's bridle. "Right nice horse you have there, son," he said, pulling open the horse's mouth. "I see it's eight years old." Then he handed the bridle to a nearby man and ordered him to lead the horse away from the crowd.

A crisis occurred in Oklahoma City on the way back from the West Coast. After Truman finished his speech explaining his stand against the Soviet Union, he learned that there was no money to get his train out of the station. Fortunately, Governor Roy J. Turner and Elmer Harbor of Shawnee, Oklahoma, held a collection party aboard the train and raised sufficient money to pay for the rest of that tour. A collapse had been averted, though it showed Truman how precarious his entire campaign was.

While he continued eastward, Governor Dewey was proceeding according to his plan. Assured that he could not lose, he did not work hard, rising late each day and limiting his speeches. Nor did he utter more than generalities, in order not to antagonize any part of his supposedly large majority. He told one audience, "Our streams should abound with fish"; another, "You know that your future lies ahead of you." Reporters noted that his campaign operated with clockwork efficiency; Truman's with a casual and uncertain air. Once when some boys threw tomatoes at Dewey's train, his press secretary told reporters the exact number thrown.

Now it was the beginning of October and Truman returned to Washington to handle Presidential business. While at the White House, he decided to send Chief Justice Fred Vinson to Moscow to deal directly with Stalin over the many issues of the Cold War. Unfriendly newspapers learned of the proposed Vinson Mission and attacked Truman for bypassing the State Department. Truman dropped the idea when Secretary of State Marshall protested. When Truman started on his eastern campaign swing, he found himself under jibing attack from Republicans, who called the Vinson Mission a campaign stunt of a desperate man.

As the campaign raced into its final weeks, reporters began to wonder why Truman drew larger crowds than Dewey, often three times as large in the same city. Moreover, Dewey's train moved quietly from one stop to the next, while Truman's train found hand-wavers alongside the tracks in the stretches between towns. "Could we be wrong?" Bob Albright of the Washington *Post* asked fellow reporters. Another reporter wrote that the people seemed "willing to give Truman anything he wanted except the Presidency." The reporters were puzzled by Truman's larger crowds, but they remained about eight to one in their belief that Dewey would win.

The price of corn dropped from $2.36 a bushel to a low of $1.38 on October 15. Republicans grew slightly concerned at the applause Truman drew when he told Midwesterners that the Republican 80th Congress was to blame. They were also concerned because of an incident at Beaucoup, Illinois, when the engineer of Dewey's train suddenly backed the train into the crowd listening to Dewey speak from the back platform. Miraculously, everyone got off the tracks in time and no one was injured. Dewey, who had almost been jerked off the platform, said "That's the first lunatic I've had for an engineer." The Republicans were aghast when union leaders said this proved that Dewey was antilabor.

Audiences continued to welcome Truman by the thousands at every stop as the campaign moved into its final period. More than 300,000 greeted him at Chicago and he drew 50,000 persons at an Indianapolis rally on a frosty evening.

"We have the Republicans on the run. We are going to win!" he cried. Reporters said that few believed this, but that audiences admired his scrappiness.

On October 31, his plane landed at Kansas City, his campaign over, and he started off by car for Independence. With a noisy police escort, reporters hurried after him. However, when they reached Delaware Street, he wasn't there. He finally arrived several minutes later and a reporter asked him why he was late. "Oh," he replied, "we were stopped by a police car and had to pull over. Seems there were some very important people going through town."

Election day, November 2, dawned and final predictions flooded the papers and magazines as Truman left home to vote. Drew Pearson informed his readers, "I surveyed the closely knit group around Tom Dewey who will take over the White House 86 days from now." The November 1 issue of *Life* ran a picture of Dewey and his wife aboard a small ship and the caption beneath read: "The next President travels by ferry boat over the broad waters of San Francisco Bay."

That evening when the first returns came in, the Republicans were preparing for a victory celebration at the Hotel Roosevelt in New York. The crowd was large and almost all campaign reporters were present to hear Dewey's expected victory speech. The Democrats were at the Biltmore Hotel and except for a few gloomy Democratic Party workers and some cub reporters the place was deserted. The four radio networks sent out alerts to member stations to prepare for Dewey's victory statement at nine P.M. Even the head of the Secret Service had quietly joined the Dewey party to protect the nation's next President.

In Missouri, Truman had slipped away to the Elms Hotel at Excelsior Spring. In the quiet of his room he heard the first small returns that showed he was in the lead. Commentators insisted things would change before long. Then at midnight he heard H. V. Kaltenborn, the famous radio newsman, say, "Mr. Truman is still ahead but these returns are from a few cities. When the returns come in from the country the result will show Dewey winning overwhelmingly." Truman then turned off the radio and fell asleep.

Later Truman still held the lead even though Dewey won New York. Dewey needed Ohio, Illinois and California to move ahead, but in the early morning hours Truman stayed ahead in returns from those states. By one A.M. the Republicans at the Hotel Roosevelt had lost their victory spark, though Herbert Brownell, Dewey's manager, pale and nervous, said in a shaky voice that Dewey would still win. A reporter described Dr. George Gallup, whose reputation as a polltaker was at stake, as resembling "an animal eating its young."

By two A.M., the large group of reporters deserted the Republican headquarters and went to the Democratic gathering at the Biltmore, where the scene was now one of anticipation. At four o'clock, James Rowley, a Secret Service man, broke into Truman's room and told him to listen to the radio. Truman learned he was 2,000,000 votes ahead, yet Kaltenborn kept insisting, "I don't see how Truman can be elected."

The most exciting election in American history ended at 11:14 A.M. when Dewey conceded that he had lost. Truman's total was 304 electoral votes to Dewey's 189.

Republican Senator Arthur Vandenberg of Michigan summed up Truman's victory in these words: "Everyone had counted him out but he came up fighting and won the battle. That's the kind of courage the American people admire."

20

---◆---

HARDEST JOB IN THE
WORLD

Pʀᴇsɪᴅᴇɴᴛ Tʀᴜᴍᴀɴ's inauguration on January 20, 1949, was the climax of a political career that began in 1906 when he served as his father's clerk in the Grandview precinct elections judging. This was an opulent inauguration, thanks to the Republican 80th Congress which had appropriated a large sum of money for the glittering Dewey inauguration it had anticipated.

Truman started his important day with an early breakfast with the ninety-seven survivors of Battery D. He told them they must not be boisterous because they were to serve as his guard of honor, marching alongside his car from the Capitol back to the White House reviewing stand for the afternoon parade.

A crowd of 100,000 watched him being sworn into office at noon and afterward he made his inaugural address. In enumerating his Four-Point foreign policy, he listened to long applause on Point Four, his proposal to provide American aid to underdeveloped countries. British historian Arnold Toynbee remarked that when Point Four was implemented it would be remembered as "the signal achievement of the age."

After the inauguration parade, the Trumans moved into Blair House across Pennsylvania Avenue. This was necessary because of the sad condition of the White House. Once when Truman was eating breakfast, he noticed that the floor shook. Another time the floor sagged while he was in the bathtub. Investigation proved that the structure built for John Adams' occupancy in 1800 was a rotting hulk, with the bottom of the building sliding into a swamp. Heavy ceilings were supported by bent, rusty nails. At Truman's urging, Congress established a Committee on Renovation, which decided to preserve the Executive Mansion's exterior but rebuild the entire interior at a cost of $5,400,000.

Shortly after his inauguration, Truman delivered his State of the Union Message. In this message to Congress, he provided a slogan for his "must" program when he said, "Every segment of our population and every individual has the right to expect from our government a fair deal." His Fair Deal consisted of twenty-four proposals for broad welfare legislation, and he hoped that the new 81st Congress with its Democratic majority would enact his Fair Deal into law.

He was to find, however, that the Democratic 81st Congress was as uncooperative as the Republican 80th Congress on domestic legislation. "I may even get on the train again and make another tour of the country," he warned Congress. His sole Fair Deal victory came with the passage of his low-cost public housing bill and it passed only because Republican Senator Taft promoted it. His proposal for a humane law to permit displaced persons who were victims of Naziism and Communism to enter the United States brought on a year and a half of fighting with Congress before it passed.

Despite his troubles with Congress, friends noted a change in Truman following his 1948 victory. He had a self-confidence and poise that he lacked before, and gave the impression he liked his crushing job. Charlie Ross said that sixty-five-year-old Truman "put in a sixteen to eighteen hour day and was fresher at the end than I was at the beginning."

After six and a half hours of sleep, he rose at 5:30 A.M., shaved, dressed and read a half-dozen morning papers. Then at seven he set off on a two-mile hike through Washington streets at his normal pace of 120 steps a minute. His hike ended at the White House where he went first to the gym and then swam twelve laps, or a quarter mile, in the indoor pool. Afterward he returned to Blair House for breakfast with his family. Sometimes before he went back to his White House office at 8:30, he wrote letters in longhand. These brought him poor publicity on occasion because he frankly wrote what was on his mind, and did not hold strong letters a day or two to reconsider whether to send them.

For a half hour at his seven-foot-wide desk, he began his work day by dictating letters to his secretary. His desk held a telephone, a three-sided gadget which had "The Buck Stops Here" printed on it, a small engraved cut of the Chicago *Tribune* headline reading DEWEY DEFEATS TRUMAN, six desk calendars, four clocks, his engagement list for the day, a Cabinet folder and a hinged, leather-bound book containing work material for his staff aides. "If I disturbed anything on his desk," said Ross, "he always put it back exactly where it had been."

After finishing dictation, Truman examined his most pressing problems until ten o'clock when he met with his staff for about forty-five minutes. These were informal meetings where he passed out assignments and discussed White House work. Then came a briefing on national and international security problems by top officials of the National Security Council.

From eleven A.M. until one P.M. and from three until four-fifteen, his time was taken up by the day's visitors, each of whom was granted a maximum of fifteen minutes. Visitors had to present in advance a written report on the subject to be discussed. Truman was a listener who did not dominate the conversation and while each of the week's one hundred visitors talked, he made marginal notes on their reports. On the report of one self-important individual, Truman wrote, "Baloney Peddler"; on another, "This man not only wants to run the country but the universe and the entire Milky Way." If he decided action was necessary on a problem discussed by a visitor, he sent the annotated report to the proper government official.

In addition to staff meetings and hours devoted to visitors and mulling over his problems, Truman held several scheduled conferences each week. On Monday morning he met with congressional leaders to go over legislative matters. The 12:30 slot on Mondays and Thursdays was reserved for the Secretary of State; on Tuesdays for the Secretary of Defense; and on Wednesday for the chairman of the National Security Resources Board. There was a Cabinet luncheon on Monday and a regular Cabinet meeting on Friday; a Wednesday afternoon party-politics session with William

Boyle, chairman of the Democratic National Committee; a Thursday afternoon meeting on foreign matters with the National Security Council; and a Thursday question-and-answer news conference with Washington correspondents.

There were still other inroads into his time. Truman's special interest was the federal budget and he spent more hours with the Budget Bureau director than he did with any other government official. Then there were the many hours preparing speeches and spare minutes given here and there for signing his name about six hundred times a day, legally required for a wide variety of government documents plus replies to a few of the 3,000 letters he received daily. "One of the sorriest problems of being President," said Charlie Ross, "is the amount of time the Chief Executive has to devote to purely ceremonial matters." Day after day he had to take precious time from his work to greet delegations, such as exchange teachers or student groups.

At six P.M. Truman quit his oval office, invariably carrying a briefcase bulging with what he called his "homework." After dinner he went to his study and went through four to six inches of homework until eleven P.M. Truman was blessed with an ability to fall asleep quickly and he never worried about decisions once he made them.

His killing pace would have soon finished Truman, if he had not changed his routine on occasion. Sometimes he went to Capitol Hill for lunch with Biffle and old Senate friends. In the evening he would sit at the grand piano and play, or he would go to Constitution Hall and listen to symphonies. Then there was his continuing strong interest in history and biography and he somehow squeezed in time for these pursuits.

Often on weekends he boarded the Presidential yacht

Williamsburg for a cruise down the Potomac. Sunday morning found him swimming for fifteen minutes in the river, a sport that worried the Secret Service. But even aboard the *Williamsburg* the name-signing chore continued and paper work and mail came down from Washington by seaplane and swift cutter.

Twice each year, in February and November, he went to Key West, Florida, for vacations. Here at the naval reservation he swam, loafed, lay in the sun, played horseshoes and wore loud sportshirts. He brought Biffle, Chief Justice Vinson and other old friends to Key West with him and he revealed an extraordinary memory reciting literary, historic and Biblical quotations as well as Latin epigrams. Charlie Ross said, "He could quote at length from Byron and Longfellow."

The Presidency was a lonely business. Truman could sail down the Potomac on weekends, rest at Key West, walk through trains when he traveled and shake hands with everyone aboard, attend the opening baseball game of the American League or occasionally participate in the activities of his Masonic lodge. But his oppressive duties and responsibilities and decision-making were always his and his alone.

21

KOREA

ALL THE WHILE Truman was urging his Fair Deal program
on Congress, his chief concentration lay in the field of foreign affairs. His Truman Doctrine of 1947 had saved Greece
and Turkey from becoming Soviet satellites; the Marshall
Plan was working beyond expectations in reviving Western
European economies; and the Berlin Airlift had forced Stalin
to give up his plan to push the United States out of Berlin.

However, Truman was still not satisfied that the United
States was doing as much as she could to contain Communism. In 1947, he had seen the U.S.S.R. seize Hungary and
then swallow Czechoslovakia the following winter. Truman
now believed that only a united and well-organized military
stand would keep Stalin from attempting similar coups in
other European countries.

In March 1948, Belgium, Holland, Luxembourg, Britain
and France had agreed to the Brussels Alliance. This was a
mutual assistance pact declaring that if any of these countries

were attacked, the other members would come to her aid. Truman realized that this was only a paper agreement because these countries were weak militarily. But if the Brussels Alliance were expanded to include other Western European countries and the United States, the total would make a significant checking power to thwart Soviet expansion.

That spring he sent State Department officials to Europe to explore this idea with interested nations. The result was the creation of the North Atlantic Treaty Organization (NATO) covering the Brussels Alliance Powers, the United States, Canada, Norway, Denmark, Iceland, Italy and Portugal. Then to implement the paper treaty Congress agreed to the Mutual Defense Assistance Act of 1949 to establish a strong and united NATO military deterrent power. There was a bitter Senate fight whether to commit American troops to Europe as part of the NATO forces, but Truman considered this essential and it was finally approved. To make certain the NATO military organization would get off to a good start, Truman appointed experienced and popular General Eisenhower as Supreme Commander for the Allied Powers in Europe.

Another vital measure was the implementation of the Point Four program to aid the underdeveloped countries of South America, Asia, Africa and the Middle East. "More than half the people of the world are living in conditions approaching misery," Truman pointed out. The Point Four program was to be based on self-help of the receiving nations with guidance by American experts.

By the end of 1950, hundreds of American industrial, scientific, medical and educational experts were at work on a hundred technical cooperation projects in twenty-seven countries. In the Shan States of Burma, for example, Point

Four technicians cut the malaria rate from 50 to 10 percent. School systems popped up for the first time in the Middle East, Asia and Latin America.

It was Truman's hope that the United Nations would accept the American proposal for international control and inspection of atomic energy production. However, the Soviet Union would not agree and in September 1949 Truman learned the reason. That month the Russians exploded their first atomic bomb and gave notice to the rest of the world that she planned to create an immense striking force of these bombs. At this time, American nuclear physicists were talking about the possibility of creating an even more devastating weapon, the thermonuclear H-bomb, which would operate by "fusion" instead of fission and have an explosive force at least a thousand times more powerful than an atomic bomb.

Truman gave serious thought to the production of the H-bomb, but dropped the idea when a top committee of scientists under Dr. Vannevar Bush recommended against it. However, when Russian production of A-bombs expanded and the Soviet Union boasted that it would soon have the H-bomb, he once more considered the subject. The Washington *Post* said his decision "may be the most cosmic that has confronted any chief of state in American history."

Truman finally ordered the H-bomb project to begin in January 1950. Whatever the cost, for self-protection the United States had to remain ahead of the Russians in the arms race. "I would have been more than happy," said Truman, "if our plan for international control had been carried out."

Another difficult problem Truman faced at this time was what to do about China. American relations with this ancient land had been cordial ever since the United States first established diplomatic and commercial relations with her in the nineteenth century. During World War II, Roosevelt had elevated China to the status of a major power, even though Japanese troops commanded much of the country and her economy was of the most primitive sort.

Truman had hardly taken office when he realized that "China was only a geographic expression" and not a united country. Chiang Kai-shek's Nationalist Government ruled only in the southwestern edge of China; the Communist forces of Mao Tse-tung held north China with a fourth of the country's population; the Russians, who had entered the Asiatic war only days before Japan surrendered, controlled Manchuria; and the great eastern and middle regions of China were a vacuum created by Japan's defeat.

The entire country was soon in turmoil with the Nationalists and Communists engaging in bitter civil war while the Russians dismantled Manchuria's factories for shipment to the U.S.S.R. General Albert C. Wedemeyer, military adviser to Chiang, reported to Truman that "the Chinese people have many grievances concerning their treatment by warlords and unscrupulous, incompetent officials." He pointed out that the weary people were 95 percent illiterate, desired only peace and had no interest in the political doctrines of either side in the civil war. In addition, Wedemeyer noted that neither side was "democratic in spirit, or intentions."

Despite this and other reports, Truman believed that the United States should lend a hand to China in her troubles. He knew that if the United States did nothing then the Russians would provide the Communists with sufficient supplies to gain control of the entire country. As an alternative, he could send a large force of American soldiers to fight alongside Chiang's army against the Communists. But this might possibly put millions of Americans into China's civil war with expected casualties that could be upward of a million youths. Even if he had wanted to do this he could not because Congress had ordered the demobilization of most of the Army and what remained was already committed to Japan and Europe.

To Truman, the only plausible alternative was to support Chiang Kai-shek while striving for a mediated truce with the Chinese Reds. So on December 1945, he sent General Marshall to China to see what he could do to end the civil war and win an agreement from the Communists to become a minority party in a unified government. Truman's gamble was that once this was accomplished, large-scale American aid would help eliminate China's poverty and Communism would then lose its appeal. "There was no reason," he said, "why the Nationalist Government could not be successful if it attended to the fundamental needs of the people."

Marshall met with initial success by getting both sides to agree to a cease-fire. But the truce was soon violated and by mid-1946 fighting became general, and by the end of the year he abandoned his mission with a blast at both sides.

During the next two years Truman saw to it that Chiang received $2 billion in American aid. But several of his generals sold their American arms and food to the Communists, other generals were inept fighters and the Chiang government made no effort to improve economic conditions in the area it controlled. As a result, in December 1949, Chiang and the remnants of his forces fled from China to the island of Formosa.

Truman underwent bitter attacks charging him with not doing enough to maintain Chiang Kai-shek in China. But as Republican Senator Arthur Vandenberg put it, "If we had made ourselves responsible for the army of the Nationalist Government, we would be in the China war for keeps. I am sure this would have jeopardized our own national security beyond any possibility of justification."

A most unfortunate result of the Communist take-over in China was that it whetted Stalin's appetite for further conquests in the Far East. At the Cairo Conference in 1943, Roosevelt, Churchill and Chiang Kai-shek had held meetings regarding the future of the peninsula of Korea, which had lain under Japanese yoke almost forty years. Their decision was that Korea should once more become a free nation after a period of big power trusteeship to prepare her for self-government.

When Truman became President, his military advisers informed him that there would not be sufficient American military forces to accept the surrender of the large Japanese army in Korea. So at Potsdam, he agreed that the Russians should handle the surrender above an arbitrary point—the 38th parallel—and the United States, below. Then both parts of Korea were to be united under big power trusteeship.

However, once the Japanese surrendered, the Russians showed their true intentions by sealing North Korea at the 38th parallel with a large, armed military force. That December, Truman sent Secretary of State Byrnes to Moscow to thresh out this agreement violation. Surprisingly, Stalin assented to a joint commission to establish a provisional Korean government composed of "Korean democratic and social organizations." Byrnes, who had little training in diplomacy, naïvely failed to define this expression. He returned convinced that he had settled the Korean problem, but Truman scolded him for "babying the Soviets," and it was the beginning of the end of Byrnes's Cabinet career.

The Joint Commission was established, but Truman's worst fears were borne out when the Russians argued that Korean democratic and social organizations meant only those who did not oppose Communism. No other groups, said the Russians, could participate in the provisional Korean government. The result was that the Joint Commission collapsed in May 1946.

Unrest developed in South Korea because that section was agricultural and lacked industries, which were almost entirely located in the North. Despite American economic aid, the situation grew distressing. Floods and strikes and a widespread blackmarket produced great inflation. Efforts by the American military commander, General John R. Hodge, to put into force a Korean counterpart of the American Bill of Rights brought charges that he was attempting to promote Communism. Furthermore, elderly Syngman Rhee, a Princeton graduate and Korean patriot, had returned to Korea after many years in exile and he conducted a continual campaign for war to unite the country.

In 1947, Truman made another attempt to settle the vexing problem by proposing to Stalin a seven-point plan that included provision for a free election by secret ballot of a united government for Korea. When Stalin rejected his proposal, Truman requested General Marshall to ask the UN to reunite Korea because of "the inability of the two powers to reach agreement."

At the same time, he ordered General Eisenhower, Admiral William Leahy, Admiral Chester Nimitz and General Carl Spaatz to advise him on the military value of Korea. In their report of September 1947, the four said: "The

United States has little strategic interest in maintaining the present troops and bases in Korea. The corps of two divisions, totaling some 45,000 men, now maintained in South Korea, could well be used elsewhere."

On the basis of this report, Truman now made a specific proposal to the UN, requesting elections in the two zones of Korea by the end of March 1948. With the establishment of a unified national government, both the Americans and the Russians would then withdraw their troops.

Not long afterward the UN established a Temporary Commission on Korea to supervise free elections. However, the Russians refused to cooperate. As they viewed it, there were ten million people in North Korea and twenty million in South Korea, which to their strange way of thinking meant that the United States would then be in control of the entire area, both North and South. Furthermore, the continuation of unrest was to the advantage of the Communists, who believed that general disorder would force the population to turn to them for relief.

As a result, the Russians would not permit the UN Commission to cross the 38th parallel, and the Commission was limited to holding an election in South Korea. On May 10, 1948, seven million South Koreans went to the polls and elected a National Assembly, which wrote a constitution and selected Syngman Rhee as President of the Republic of Korea. In August, when Truman recognized Rhee, the American military government came to an end. In the North, the Russians countered by announcing the establishment of a dictatorship called the "Democratic People's Republic of Korea."

Truman had no intention of leaving the new ROK (Republic of Korea) to its own limited resources. On the military side, he ordered American equipment and training of a 65,000-man ROK army, coast guard and police force. In addition, he shipped the Rhee government a billion dollars of economic aid, despite widespread congressional opposition to what some Congressmen called a "black, bottomless hole."

By 1950, Truman was displeased with Rhee's lack of interest in democratizing South Korea or in improving the lot of the people. Said Truman, Rhee had "attracted to himself men of extreme right-wing attitudes" who used inhuman methods "to break up political meetings and control political enemies." However, Truman believed that the United States had no authority to meddle with the internal affairs of other nations. He realized that Korea was hardly a showcase for democracy, nor did it have strategic value to the United States. Yet as the Republic's creator, the United States was directly responsible for maintaining her existence.

That spring the Central Intelligence Agency reported to Truman that following the Communist conquest of China there appeared to be a buildup of military strength in North Korea. But the CIA also reported a strengthening of Red military power in a dozen other areas in the world. To send American soldiers to bolster South Korea meant weakening other American positions, and in the absence of more precise information there was little to be gained by such action.

On June 24, 1950, Truman dedicated the new Friendship Airport at Baltimore and then flew to Independence for a quiet weekend at home. At ten-thirty that evening Secretary of State Dean Acheson, who had succeeded General Marshall, called him in great agitation. Acheson informed him that North Koreans had invaded South Korea. When Truman told him he would fly back to Washington immediately, Acheson replied that there was still not sufficient information to determine whether this was an all-out invasion or merely a skirmish. Truman agreed with Acheson's suggestion that the United States request the UN Security Council to meet at once and declare that an act of aggression had been committed.

Early the next afternoon Acheson called him again to report that the North Koreans were making a massive effort to conquer South Korea. Truman's face was grim when his plane landed at Washington at 7:15 P.M., and he held a long meeting with his advisers at Blair House. Acheson reported that the UN Security Council had voted 9–0 for a resolution calling for an end of the fighting and the withdrawal of North Korean troops behind the 38th parallel. Had the Russians been present, they would have vetoed this resolution. But some time before, when the UN had refused to seat Red China, the Russian delegates had stalked out of the Security Council.

To Truman, the Security Council's resolution was weak because it did not suggest any counterthreat to the invaders if they did not quit South Korea. For the time being, Truman ordered General MacArthur, then Supreme Commander in occupied Japan, to evacuate the 2,000 Americans in South Korea and to supply arms to the ROK forces by airdrop.

Only sad news regarding South Korea crossed Truman's desk the following day. His military advisers had spoken glowingly about the fighting capacity of the ROK army, but they were retreating in disorder now and Rhee's government had fled from the capital city of Seoul to Taegu, 150 miles to the south. Truman held another military conference that evening and ordered Secretary of Defense Louis Johnson to instruct MacArthur to support Rhee with American air and naval forces. Truman made no mention of American ground forces.

On the following day Acheson won a stronger resolution from the UN Security Council. This new resolution called on member nations to "furnish such assistance to the Republic of Korea as may be necessary to repel the armed attack."

Two nights later MacArthur called the Joint Chiefs of Staff at the Pentagon. He had gone to Korea to observe the fighting firsthand. Half the ROK army was gone and the rest were in full retreat. The only way to prevent a collapse of South Korea," he said, was to commit "U.S. ground combat forces into the Korean battle area."

Secretary of the Army Frank Pace awakened Truman at five A.M. to tell him of the MacArthur conversation. A major decision faced Truman: Was the United States to go to war over a piece of territory that had little strategic value to her and for a government that would not install the basic operating principles of a democracy? Yet if he took no action, the Communists would assume they could invade other countries without fear of American action. In addition, if the Communists were not stopped in Korea, the UN, which had called for action by member nations, would no doubt collapse.

Truman did not hesitate. "Inform General MacArthur that the use of one regimental combat team is approved," he told Pace. And thus began the American and UN war in Korea.

MacArthur's initial forces thrown against the North Koreans were outnumbered 100 to one. Yet he reasoned that if he could trick the enemy into believing he possessed a large army, he could hold them off until further American units arrived. "I threw in troops by air in the hopes I could rally the fast-retreating South Korean forces," he said. "I also hoped by that arrogant display to fool the enemy into a belief that I had greater resources at my disposal than I did. The enemy could not understand that we could make such an effort with such a small force. We gained ten days by that process." During those precious days MacArthur gained the time he needed to bring in two additional divisions from Japan and deploy them around Pusan, at the heel of the peninsula.

Throughout August, after the North Koreans learned they had been outwitted, they put up a strong assault to push the Americans into the sea beyond Pusan. The fighting was so fierce and so discouraging that many Senators took to ridiculing Truman for labeling the war a "police action." Some demanded a withdrawal to Japan and the abandonment of Korea. Others called for the firing of Secretary of State Acheson because he had said in January that America's first-line defense perimeter did not include Korea. But Truman stoutly defended Acheson, pointing out that in the same speech his Secretary had also said, "Should such an attack occur, the initial reliance must be on the people attacked, and then upon the commitments of the entire civilized world under the Charter of the UN."

It was MacArthur who turned what appeared to be a total defeat into a brilliant victory. In mid-August, while the Americans stubbornly held on to the Pusan beachhead, Truman sent General J. Lawton Collins and Admiral Forrest Sherman to discuss strategy with him. What MacArthur proposed was a daring amphibious landing all the way around the peninsula to Inchon on the west coast near Seoul close to the 38th parallel. The North Koreans pounding at the gates of Pusan would never expect an attack so far to their rear. Then he could cut the enemy's supply lines and trap all the North Koreans below the parallel.

Collins and Sherman showed little enthusiasm for MacArthur's proposal. Inchon was too far behind Pusan, they insisted, to relieve that last American stronghold on Korea. Furthermore, Inchon was a dangerous landing place, for offshore tides there rose and fell twenty feet. A landing was possible only at high tide, giving ships only a few hours before being caught in mud extending two miles from shore. Kunsan, only halfway back to the 38th parallel, was a safer spot for a surprise attack, they said.

But MacArthur would not agree to their proposal. "Inchon will save 100,000 lives," he told them, "while Kunsan would not sever the enemy's supply lines and would therefore serve little purpose."

The decision was left to Truman, who considered the Inchon plan "a daring strategic conception" and gave his quick approval.

It was on September 15, 1950, when the first Marine assault came ashore at Inchon. Then the X Corps under General Edward Almond struck toward Seoul and freed the ROK capital on September 28. Not long afterward, General Walton Walker's 8th Army at faroff Pusan noticed that North Korean pressure was noticeably weaker. When the North Koreans attempted to head north, they found their supply lines slashed. Then caught in a vise between the X Corps and the 8th Army, the invaders collapsed and 130,000 surrendered.

MacArthur soon had all of South Korea cleared and from Washington Truman sent his Commander, who was now also Commander in Chief of the UN Forces in Korea, a congratulatory message. "Few operations in military history can match either the delaying action where you traded space for time or the brilliant maneuver which has now resulted in the liberation of Seoul . . . Well and nobly done."

With the clearing of South Korea, Truman now faced a new problem. Should he declare the Korean action at an end? Or should he send MacArthur north of the 38th parallel to liberate North Korea?

When the invasion first began, Truman had favored only the chasing of the North Koreans from the territory south of the parallel. But now, after deliberation, he gave Mac-Arthur a new military objective—"the destruction of the North Korean Armed Forces." As he put it: "We have to go beyond the 38th parallel to convince the North Koreans they are vanquished and that further aggression does not pay."

Before MacArthur started North, he twice appealed to the North Koreans to surrender and cooperate in establishing "a unified, independent and democratic government." When they ignored his appeals, he sent the X Corps and the 8th Army across the parallel despite a warning from Chou En-lai, the Foreign Minister of Red China, that his country "will not stand idly by and see North Korea invaded."

Shortly after the drive northward began, Truman decided to make the personal acquaintance of MacArthur and requested him to fly to Wake Island for a meeting on October 15. When the *Independence* braked to a halt on Wake at six A.M. that day, MacArthur was already there and Truman said, shaking his hand, "I've been a long time meeting you."

There were several vexing problems that Truman wished to discuss with MacArthur; and they rode immediately in a squeaky jalopy, the best car on the island, to a Quonset hut for a private conference. An hour later the two men went to another building for a 7:30 A.M. conference with staff aides. Here they discussed the proposed Japanese peace treaty, the postwar rebuilding of Korea and a Pacific pact similar to NATO in Europe.

At one point Truman turned to MacArthur and asked, "What are the chances for Chinese or Soviet interference in the Korean fighting?"

MacArthur replied that CIA and his own intelligence unit counted about 300,000 Red Chinese troops in Manchuria, across the North Korean Yalu River boundary. However, he added, there was little chance that the Chinese would enter the fighting directly. As for Soviet intervention, he continued, the Russians could not bring in many ground soldiers before the coming winter.

Truman then asked MacArthur how long the war would last, and MacArthur replied that he expected resistance to end by Thanksgiving. When Truman landed at San Francisco on October 17, he announced, "I had a very satisfactory conference with General Douglas MacArthur."

The offensive in North Korea moved forward at a sweeping pace. On October 20, the North Korean capital of Pyongyang fell and the entire population turned out to welcome MacArthur. This bore out the general's prediction, made earlier to Truman, that the North Koreans were basically no greater admirers of Communism than South Koreans.

Truman's first inkling of trouble came on the day Pyongyang fell when the CIA reported to him that the Chinese Reds planned to cross the Yalu into Korea. Then during the last week of October, the X Corps captured some Chinese Red soldiers. MacArthur cautioned "against hasty conclusions," but Truman's concern was aroused.

On November 1, after careful consideration of the possibility of large-scale Chinese intervention in Korea, Truman

returned to Blair House at one P.M. for lunch with his wife
and mother-in-law. Afterward, he went upstairs for a nap
before proceeding to Arlington Cemetery where he was to
speak at the unveiling of a statue of British Field Marshal
Sir John Dill.

Ever since Truman moved into Blair House, while waiting
for the White House to be rebuilt, the Secret Service worried
about his safety. For the residence sat almost flush against
the sidewalk and Truman's second-floor bedroom faced the
street. Since pedestrians were not barred from the sidewalk
in front of the house, assassins could easily lob a bomb into
the building.

At 2:20 P.M. on this day, two Puerto Ricans suddenly approached Blair House, well-armed with guns and ammunition. Truman had appointed the first governor of Puerto
Rico and had fought successfully with Congress for its status
as a Commonwealth with a new constitution. However, these
two fanatics belonged to the Puerto Rican Nationalist group,
which favored complete independence from the United
States. It was their wild idea that if they could kill Truman,
the United States would be plunged into revolution, and
during the upheaval the Puerto Rican Nationalists would declare their independence.

Thirty-one shots were fired in three minutes in their attempt to gain entrance into Blair House. When Truman
heard firing, he ran to the window. A guard glanced up and
frantically yelled to him to step back. At the end of the
melee, one of the Puerto Ricans lay dead and a policeman
lay mortally wounded. Truman remained unruffled and went
to Arlington Cemetery on schedule. "A President has to
expect those things," he said.

Not long after this attempt on his life, Truman learned

from MacArthur that Communist planes were crossing into North Korea from Manchuria. MacArthur requested permission to engage in "hot pursuit" of enemy planes across the Yalu. He also demanded the right to bomb Chinese ground targets. Truman realized, however, that such action would immediately extend the war to China. This would suit the USSR admirably, for as the real aggressor in Korea, she could then sit back out of the fighting and watch the United States engage in a long and costly war with China. As General Omar Bradley put it to Truman, such a conflict would involve the United States "in the wrong war, at the wrong place, at the wrong time and with the wrong enemy." As a result, Truman denied MacArthur the right of "hot pursuit" and the permission to bomb Chinese territory.

Bound by these restrictions, MacArthur, nevertheless, began a renewed drive to reach the Yalu River. On November 21, he reported to Truman that small units under his command had arrived at the border. Three days later when he sent General Walker's 8th Army on what he expected would be the final offensive, he said, "This should for all practical purposes end the war and restore peace and unity to Korea."

But on November 26, MacArthur's hope for complete victory evaporated. Under cover of darkness, 200,000 well-armed Chinese Communist soldiers marched across the Yalu bridges into North Korea. Two days later, the 8th Army and the X Corps were hit by massive assaults. Easy victory at the Yalu was now reversed in a headlong retreat and a fight for survival.

On December 5, while Truman met with British Prime Minister Attlee over the issue of the possible use of the atomic bomb in the Far East, Charlie Ross died suddenly. Truman was stunned and grief-stricken by the death of his boyhood friend but insisted on going to Constitution Hall that evening to hear his daughter Margaret in a concert. Early the next morning when he read a tasteless review of Margaret's concert in the Washington *Post,* he became furious. Without breakfast, mourning the loss of Ross, and with both Attlee and a military catastrophe on his hands, he wrote a wrathful longhand letter on a White House pad to the music critic.

The publication of the letter brought widespread editorial denunciation of the Presidential temper. Truman was mollified to some extent when General Marshall told him, "The only thing that music critic didn't criticize was the varnish on the piano."

As the dreary days of December crawled along, the news from Korea continued disheartening. By January 4, the Reds had pushed below the 38th parallel and captured Seoul. Even though MacArthur was able to regroup his forces seventy miles below the parallel, the Joint Chiefs of Staff warned Truman to expect a reenactment of the Pusan beachhead stand of the previous August and perhaps a retreat to Japan. But by March, MacArthur's men were back at the 38th parallel.

A crisis now befell Truman when MacArthur insisted that all of Korea must be set free. However, he could not proceed far beyond the 38th parallel because of Truman's earlier orders barring bombing of Chinese supply bases and chasing enemy planes across the Chinese border. Unless the President dropped these restrictions, MacArthur complained, all that was left to him was an "accordion war," with one side advancing until it overextended its supply lines and then the other side taking the offensive until it, too, moved ahead of its supplies.

On March 7, 1951, MacArthur again asked for an expansion of the war by issuing a statement to reporters. This time he proposed a blockade of the Chinese coast, air bombardment of her industrial centers, the use of Chiang Kai-shek's Formosan forces in Korea and an invasion of South China by Chiang's army. It was MacArthur's belief that the Communists were so poorly established in China that they would not be able to retaliate and would hence suffer quick defeat.

Truman was deeply disturbed by MacArthur's statement, for he was making his first moves to negotiate a cease-fire in Korea. The clearing of South Korea had enabled him to make this proposal on the basis of strength. But MacArthur's statement was making it appear that the United States actually courted World War III.

Truman was also disturbed by another MacArthur statement on March 24. Again MacArthur threatened to expand the war to China's "coastal areas and interior bases." He also demanded that North Korea surrender to him personally.

"By this act," Truman said, "MacArthur left me no choice —I could no longer tolerate his insubordination." For if he did, he would have relinquished his Constitutional oath and handed over civilian control of the government to the military branch. Under the Constitution, the President is in charge of the military and civilian activities in the Executive branch, and the public servants employed in the agencies serve only at his pleasure. Hence, MacArthur's duty was to carry out the policy of the President and not to force the President to accept the changes he desired. Therefore, when MacArthur attempted to dictate policy, he was in direct violation of the intent of the Constitution.

The final climax came on April 5 when Truman learned that MacArthur had written a critical letter about his policy to House Minority Leader Joseph Martin. MacArthur's insubordination could no longer be tolerated.

At one A.M. on April 11, after lengthy sessions with his military advisers, Truman called a special news conference. "With deep regret," he announced, "I have concluded that General MacArthur is unable to give his wholehearted support to the policies of the U.S. Government in matters pertaining to his official duties." With that, he relieved MacArthur of his commands and selected Lieutenant General Matthew Ridgway to succeed him.

After recalling MacArthur, Truman continued his efforts to effect a cease-fire in Korea. Finally on June 23, 1951, the Soviet Government announced that it favored a negotiated armistice, and on July 7, liaison officers from both sides met in a tent at Kaesong, near the 38th parallel.

By 1952, Truman believed that a satisfactory agreement would soon be made. But when the Communists suddenly demanded the return of all prisoners, including those who did not want to return to North Korea, he refused to agree. "We will not buy an armistice by turning over human beings for slaughter or slavery," he said.

As a result, the truce negotiations continued without success throughout the rest of Truman's term in office. And while they continued, the fighting went on at a cost of 80,000 American casualties.

22

MR. CITIZEN

WHEN 1952 arrived, Democratic leaders insisted that Truman run again. But Truman bluntly asserted that he "didn't want to be carried out of the White House in a casket." His years as President had been long and arduous and he believed that the Democratic Party had several able younger men capable of providing the country with excellent leadership.

Truman's waning period in office was particularly difficult. There was first the continuing failure of the Korean truce negotiations because of the ruthless Communist demand for forcible repatriation of prisoners. The American public was showing great unrest at the seemingly insoluble war. Despite general agreement that Truman had acted courageously in meeting the Communist challenge, mounting casualty lists evoked emotional charges that Truman was personally responsible for a "needless" loss of life. There is little question that by 1952, Americans considered the Korean action the most unpopular war in history. It was not until the following year, when Truman was out of office, and upon the death of Stalin, that the new Soviet rulers announced themselves in favor of voluntary repatriation.

The failure of the Korean truce negotiations was only one of a long list of events that made Truman's last year difficult. Late in 1951, a nation-wide steel strike threatened when steel companies refused to accept the recommendation of the Federal Wage Stabilization Board for a wage increase among factory workers. Because a shutdown would seriously affect the supply of military equipment to Korea and the NATO forces in Europe, Truman ordered a governmental seizure of 92 steel mills. A charge by the industry that he had exceeded his Constitutional powers brought on a hectic seven-months' newspaper tirade against Truman that ended in July 1952 when the Supreme Court handed down its opinion. When the Court ruled that he had acted unconstitutionally, a seven-week strike by steelworkers followed.

There was also his long fight in 1952 with Southern Democrats from the oil states, who wanted the federal government to turn over its control of oil deposits in the continental shelf below the sea to the states. A bill to this effect passed Congress, but Truman promptly vetoed it, charging, "It would have been a gift to three states at the expense of the other forty-five." As a result, oil state politicians vowed they would vote Republican in 1952.

Equally vexing to Truman were the many instances of wrongdoing uncovered among lesser officials in his Administration. The opposition loudly lumped all such findings under the title of the "Truman Scandals," despite the fact that he was not personally involved. A Senate Committee found that several employees of the Reconstruction Finance Corporation had accepted bribes and gifts in negotiating loans to private firms. Then several officials of the Bureau of Internal Revenue were caught in dubious tax settlement maneuvers. Some were discovered to have failed to file their own tax statements!

Truman ordered the firing of a dozen top Internal Revenue officers, 200 less important employees and forced the Attorney General to resign. On March 29, 1952, he explained to the American people: "I stand for honest government. I have worked for it . . . I hate corruption because it is the deadly enemy of all the things the Democratic Party has been doing all these years. I hate corruption everywhere, but I hate it most of all in a Democratic officeholder." To the charge that the entire federal government's 3,000,000 employees were dishonest, he said, "I'm disgusted with these efforts to discredit and blacken the character and reputation of the whole federal service."

At the beginning of 1952, Truman combed the field for his successor. His first choice was Chief Justice Fred Vinson, but Vinson rejected the offer of support by disclosing his poor physical condition. By a process of elimination, Truman then decided that Governor Adlai E. Stevenson of Illinois would make the ablest Democratic nominee for Chief Executive.

At first, Stevenson took himself out of contention and Truman asked Supreme Court Justice William Douglas to run. Douglas also turned him down. But by the time the Democratic National Convention began in July, Stevenson changed his mind and became the Democratic nominee.

Truman campaigned vigorously for Stevenson. But he was not surprised when General Eisenhower, who had accepted the Republican nomination, defeated Stevenson by more than six million votes on November 4. For Eisenhower's popularity had not waned since his World War II duty in defeating Hitler's Germany.

Although Truman had been hurt by the Republican campaign, which had been directed against him personally rather than on a higher plane of the issues of the day, he forgot about this after the election. He offered full cooperation with the incoming Administration in order that government operations not be jarred during the changeover. He invited Eisenhower to visit him for a briefing and he told his aides to work closely with the men who would replace them.

On January 15, 1953, Truman made his final report to the people in a television and radio address. He recalled his deep emotions on that late afternoon in April 1945 when he succeeded Roosevelt. Then he reviewed in detail the major events of his eight years in office. As for the future, he declared he was fully confident that the free world would not only survive but would triumph over totalitarianism.

Shortly before noon on January 20, Truman's last action as President was to return a pad of paper to the desk of an aide. Then he joined Eisenhower for the ride to the Capitol, where the new President would take the oath of office. Afterward, a crowd of 5,000 persons came to Union Station to bid Truman farewell. Truman's long political career was now over.

When Truman returned to Independence, he found that the town had become a tourist's mecca. Rain or shine, crowds gathered around the old Delaware Street house for a glimpse of "Harry," as they addressed the former President. After a while, he had to put a lock on the front gate to keep people from walking into the house. On one occasion, he and Mrs. Truman slipped across the street to visit with Cousins Nellie and Ethel Noland. Almost as soon as they rapped on the door, a crowd collected at the Truman house across the way. The Trumans waited in vain for the crowd to disperse. "We had to spend most of the evening on the front porch all by ourselves," Mrs. Truman said, "because our cousins weren't at home."

As the years moved along, the loud barrage of opposition

to him by Republican editors and politicians, which had
been his steady diet in office, gradually faded. Yet in some
quarters, those who had opposed him still considered him
with strong emotion.

For instance, Truman was riding in a car to a dinner in
San Francisco when his chauffeur lost his way. Truman
climbed out and rang the doorbell of a large house to ask
for directions. "An unmistakenly Republican-looking gentleman," said Truman, "opened the door." He took a hard look
at the ex-President, stepped back and blinked his eyes. "I
hope I'm not hurting your feelings," the man said, "but you
look exactly like that old soandso Harry Truman."

"I hope I'm not hurting your feelings either," Truman
replied. "But I am that soandso."

For a time, Truman maintained an office in Kansas City,
riding along Truman Road past stores named for him—
Truman's Car Wash, Truman's Pharmacy, Harry's Tavern
and Harry's Used Furniture. At his office, Truman spent
much of his time working on his memoirs, which were published in two volumes, and which were almost entirely an
account of his Presidential years.

Then in 1957, with the dedication of the 527-foot-long
Harry S. Truman Library at the edge of Independence, he
no longer had to go to his Kansas City office. Here at the
library are stored 3.5 million documents, the papers, letters
and reports of Truman and his political associates. For the
use of students, the library also began acquiring microfilm
collections of the papers of Truman's thirty-one predecessors.

Among the displays at the library is a room which is the
exact copy of the President's White House office. In the lobby
is a mural by the renowned artist, Thomas Hart Benton,
depicting Independence's glory as the starting point of the
Santa Fe and Oregon Trails. Also in the lobby is the table

on which the UN Charter was signed in 1945; and on ex-
hibit are Truman's Fair Deal Message to Congress, photo-
graphs of the Potsdam conferees and the 1948 whistle-stop
campaign. Down the hall from Truman's office is an audi-
torium where he speaks frequently to visiting groups of high
school students on American history and answers questions
they put to him. His position is that if the youth of the
country take an interest and pride in their nation's history,
a bright future for the United States will be assured.

Truman still plays an active role in politics, traveling
about the country at campaigntime to stir up excitement for
Democratic candidates. The advancing years have not
dimmed his ability to evoke strong emotions from members
of both political parties from coast to coast, as he talks on
the issues of the day. "I expect to be cussed and discussed for
a long time," he said. However, he carefully refrains from
taking a position on foreign affairs that differs from that
of the President in office.

Interest and pride in his nation's history are the golden
chords that swept Truman along from a piano-playing youth
in the Waldo Street Gang to bank clerk, farmer, oil wildcatter, Captain Harry of Battery D, shopkeeper, savings and
loan bank president, through the years as county judge,
United States Senator, war program investigator, Vice-President and finally President.

Yet there were more ingredients than these in Truman's
political pot. For historians agree that he must be ranked
with the strongest of American Presidents. After the din of
the noisy political battles of his era are forgotten, what is
left is a man of courage who was "utterly human under
agonizing burdens." As General Marshall once evaluated
Mr. Truman: "The full measure of this man is not only the
courage of his decisions, but the integrity of them."

BIBLIOGRAPHY

Abels, Jules, *The Truman Scandals*, 1956
────── *Out of the Jaws of Victory*, 1959
Alinsky, Saul, *John L. Lewis*, 1949
Allen, George E., *Presidents Who Have Known Me*, 1960
Allen, Robert S. (and William V. Shannon), *The Truman-Merry-Go-Round*, 1950
American Guide Series: *Missouri, A Guide to the "Show Me" State*, 1941
Attlee, Clement R., *As It Happened*, 1954
Barker, John T., *Missouri Lawyer*, 1949
Barkley, Alben, *That Reminds Me*, 1954
Beach, Marjorie, *The Mayor's Wife*, 1953
Bell, Jack, *Splendid Misery*, 1960
Bendiner, Robert, *White House Fever*, 1960
Bloom, Sol, *Autobiography*, 1948
Bolles, Blair, *Men of Good Intentions*, 1960
Boorstin, Daniel J., *Genius of American Politics*, 1953
Brandeis, Louis D., *The Curse of Bigness*, 1934
Brown, A. T., *Politics of Reform*, 1958
Bryan, William Jennings, *The Memoirs of*, 1925
Bundschu, Henry A., *Harry S. Truman—The Missourian*, 1948
Burch, John P., *A True Story of Charles W. Quantrell and His Guerilla Band*, 1923
Busch, Noel F., *Adlai E. Stevenson*, 1952

Byrnes, James F., *Speaking Frankly*, 1947
———— *All in One Lifetime*, 1958
Carr, Robert K., *The House Committee on Un-American Activities, 1945–1950*, 1952
Churchill, Sir Winston, *Second World War*, 6 vols., 1948–1953
Clemens, Cyril, *Truman Speaks*, 1946
Coffin, Tris, *Missouri Compromise*, 1947
Connally, Tom, and Steinberg, Alfred, *My Name Is Tom Connally*, 1954
Coyle, David C., *Ordeal of the Presidency*, 1960
Daniels, Jonathan, *The Man of Independence*, 1950
David, Paul T. and associates, *The National Story (Presidential Nominating Politics in 1952)*, 1954
Dayton, Eldorous L., *Give 'Em Hell, Harry*, 1956
Dillon, Mary E., *Wendell Willkie*, 1952
Donovan, Robert J., *Eisenhower: The Inside Story*, 1956
Douglas, Paul H., *Economy in the National Government*, 1952
Douglass, Robert S., *History of Missouri Baptists*, 1934
Dulles, John F., *War or Peace*, 1950
Eisenhower, Dwight D., *Crusade in Europe*, 1948
Eccles, Marriner, *Beckoning Frontiers*, 1951
Farley, James A., *Behind the Ballots*, 1938
———— *Jim Farley's Story*, 1948
Feis, Herbert, *The China Tangle*, 1953
———— *Between War and Peace*, 1960
———— *Japan Subdued*, 1961
Finer, Herman, *The Presidency*, 1960
Flynn, Edward J., *You're the Boss*, 1947
Forrestal, James, and Millis, Walter, *Forrestal Diaries*, 1951
Garwood, Darrell, *Crossroads of America*, 1948
Goldman, Eric, *The Crucial Decade*, 1956
Gunther, John, *Inside USA*, 1947
Haskell, Henry C. and Fowler, Richard, *City of the Future*, 1950
Hassett, William D., *Off the Record*, 1958
Helm, William P., *Harry Truman*, 1947
Hillman, William, *Mr. President*, 1952
Hunt, Frazier, *Untold Story of Douglas MacArthur*, 1954
Hyman, Sidney, *The American President*, 1954
Ickes, Harold, *Secret Diary*, 3 vols., 1953–54
Johnson, Walter, *1600 Pennsylvania Avenue*, 1960
Koenig, Louis W., *Truman Administration*, 1956
Leahy, William D., *I Was There*, 1950
Lee, Jay M., *The Artilleryman*, 1920
Lord, Russell, *The Wallaces of Iowa*, 1947
Mayerberg, Samuel, *Chronicle of an American Crusader*, 1944

McNaughton, Frank, and Hehmeyer, Walter, *This Man Truman*, 1945
────── *Harry Truman, President*, 1948
Miller, W. H., *The History of Kansas City*, 1880
Milligan, Maurice M., *Missouri Waltz*, 1948
Missouri Crime Survey, 1926
Neustadt, Richard, *Presidential Power*, 1960
Norris, George W., *Fighting Liberal, An Autobiography*, 1945
Parkman, Francis, *The Oregon Trail*, 1849
Parrington, Vernon L., *Main Currents in American Thought*, 1926
Political History of Kansas City, 1902
Political History of Jackson County, 1902
Pollard, James E., *Presidents and the Press*, 1947
Powell, Gene, *Tom's Boy Harry*, 1948
Reddig, William M., *Tom's Town*, 1947
Redding, John M., *Inside the Democratic Party*, 1958
Richberg, Donald, *My Hero*, 1954
Rovere, Richard, and Schlesinger, Arthur M., Jr., *The General and the President*, 1952
Schauffler, Edward R., *Harry Truman—Son of the Soil*, 1947
Schlesinger, Arthur M., Jr., *Politics of Upheaval*, 1960
Sherwood, Robert E., *Roosevelt and Hopkins*, 1948
Shoemaker, Floyd C., editor, *Missouri Day by Day*, 1942
Smith, Ira, *Dear Mr. President*, 1949
Smith, Merriman, *Thank You, Mr. President*, 1946
────── *A President Is Many Men*, 1948
Spanier, J. W., *The Truman-MacArthur Controversy*, 1959
Steinberg, Alfred, *Mrs. R: The Life of Eleanor Roosevelt*, 1958
────── *Douglas MacArthur*, 1961
Stettinius, Edward R., *Roosevelt and the Russians*, 1949
Timmons, Bascom, *Garner of Texas*, 1948
Truman, Harry S., *Year of Decision*, 1955
────── *Years of Trial and Hope*, 1956
────── *Mr. Citizen*, 1960
Tully, Grace, *FDR, My Boss*, 1949
U.S. Congress, Senate, Special Committee Investigating National Defense Program, 1943–1944, 20 vols., 1944
Vandenberg, Arthur, and Vandenberg, Arthur, Jr., *Private Papers of Senator Vandenberg*, 1952
Weizmann, Chaim, *Trial and Error*, 1949
Weyl, Nathaniel, *Battle Against Disloyalty*, 1951
White, William Allen, *The Autobiography of*, 1946
Whitney, Alexander Fell, *Railroad Rules-Wage Movement in the United States*, 1946
NEWSPAPERS *The New York Times*, New York *Herald Tribune*, Wash-

ington *Post*, Washington *Star*, Washington *Times-Herald*, Chicago *Tribune*, Kansas City *Star*, Kansas City *Journal-Post*, The Independence *Examiner*, St. Louis *Post-Dispatch*, St. Louis *Globe-Democrat*, *Congressional Record*

MAGAZINES *Time*, *Newsweek*, *Life*, *Look*, *The New Yorker*, *Reader's Digest*, *Harper's*, *Atlantic Monthly*, *Forum and Century*, *Fortune*, *Collier's*, *Tomorrow*, *Common Sense*, *Foreign Service*

INDEX

THE AUTHOR

A noted political writer and journalist who has been intimately connected with the Washington scene for many years, Alfred Steinberg's articles on various aspects of politics have appeared in many major magazines. He has worked for many government and national agencies. Mr. Steinberg is the author of *Daniel Webster, Eleanor Roosevelt, Admiral Richard E. Byrd, Douglas MacArthur, Woodrow Wilson* and *John Marshall* in the Lives to Remember series. He, his wife and three children make their home in Silver Spring, Maryland.